THE UNDIVIDED SELF

BRINGING YOUR WHOLE LIFE IN LINE WITH GOD'S WILL

EARL D. WILSON

InterVarsity Press
Downers Grove
Illinois 60515

InterVarsity Press is the book-publishing division of Inter-Varsity Christian Fellowship, a student movement active on campus at hundreds of universities, colleges and schools of nursing. For information about local and regional activities, write IVCF, 233 Langdon St., Madison, WI 53703.

Distributed in Canada through InterVarsity Press, 860 Denison St., Unit 3, Markham, Ontario L3R 4H1, Canada.

All quotations from Scripture, unless otherwise noted, are taken from the Holy Bible: New International Version. *Copyright* © *1978 by the New York International Bible Society. Used by permission of Zondervan Bible Publishers.*

Cover illustration: Roberta Polfus

ISBN 0-87784-842-4

Printed in the United States of America

Library of Congress Cataloging in Publication Data

Wilson, Earl D., 1939-
    The undivided self.

    Includes bibliographical references.
    1. Christian life—1960-   I. Title.
BV4501.2.W554 1983   248.4   83-6189
ISBN 0-87784-842-4

17 16 15 14 13 12 11 10 9 8 7 6 5 4 3 2 1
95 94 93 92 91 90 89 88 87 86 85 84 83

This book is about faith and is therefore
dedicated to the two people who have taught me
the most about living by faith.
The first is my mother, Emma Reed Wilson,
who died unexpectedly in 1971.
Mom showed me that trusting God
on a day-by-day basis makes sense.
The second is my loving wife, Sandy Wilson,
who has shown me what it means
to fall in love with Jesus Christ.

My life is richer because of the influence of
these two special people.

I
Divisible
We
Stand

There once was a fox, a fine furry fellow;
But he was uptight and couldn't stay mellow.
He saw a psychologist, a sharp Ph.D.
The doctor said, "Foxie, you must learn to be."

The fox couldn't handle such fuzzy advice.
He made an appointment but didn't go twice.
His nervousness worsened. He started to twitch.
Sometimes he would moan. Other times he would itch.

One day in the forest he came up with a plan.
"I'll go see a Preacher Fox. He'll understand."
The Preacher Fox smiled, as good preachers do,
And told him, "With faith you can be made new."

Foxie, he listened, even got on his knees
And howled to the heavens a mournful, "Help, please!"
He prayed more and harder with each passing day,
But the Great God of Mammals still seemed far away.

"I can't make it work," he cried to the preacher.
"I want to be heavenly but act like a creature."
The Preacher Fox smiled and said, "Though you're tryin',
There's a part of yourself I'm afraid you're denyin'.

"I'm telling you, Foxie, your self is askew.
Do emotions or thoughts tell you what you should do?"
Little Foxie thought hard. This was no easy test.
Was he uptight the most when his mind was at rest?

Did his heart guide his actions or was it his will?
Could his life become whole again? Oh, what a thrill!
He had almost decided and found rest for his soul
When he heard a loud noise and ran back to his hole.

The allegorical verse of our dear friend Foxie reminds me of myself and others I know. Something about life seems strange to us. In fact, many days tilt more than a little.

For Todd it was uncertainty about how being a student could fit into his spiritual life. His girlfriend, Jill, was more explicit. "I just don't know how to live the way God wants me to. I seem to be in constant turmoil. I try to trust God, but some aspect or another of my life is always out of whack."

Our friend the fox became religious, but even then God seemed far away. Foxie has lots of human counterparts. He was told that he needed to learn to live by faith. It sounds simplistic, but the need is real. Todd and Jill also said they needed to trust God more. Together they agreed, "We want to but we don't know how."

A young mother came to see me at my office. She said, "I'm an emotional wreck. I just can't stay on top of things. One day I'm happy. The next day I'm crying my eyes out. One day I feel like a strong Christian, and the next day I feel overrun with doubts."

She took a few deep breaths and then asked the inevitable question, "Am I losing my mind?"

Trying not to make light of her distress, I said, "Well, if you are, then so are hundreds of other people. It sounds like you are looking for some consistency in your life."

She nodded, saying, "At times I feel like a roller coaster."

Bill's problem was a little different. He approached me at a conference and asked for some time to talk. He was a committed Christian. He wanted to study to be a pastor. His problem, however, was that he was not in control of his life. He couldn't resist sexual temptation and was being torn apart by guilt. When Bill was in control, he knew what he believed and was able to follow his beliefs. There were other times, however, when he seemed to make all the wrong decisions. It was then that his beliefs didn't seem to affect his behavior at all. He felt split apart by his own choices. He was confused and dissatisfied.

To my knowledge, during almost twenty years of professional practice as a psychological counselor, only one of my clients has committed suicide. He had been told, "When you receive Christ, you will no longer be troubled with homosexual lust." However, after one year as a believer his lustful thoughts remained. Neither Scripture nor human logic was sufficient to convince him that the initial promise was false. He was convinced that even though he had accepted Christ and turned his life over to Jesus, God had still rejected him. He was in deepest anguish because he didn't understand the relationship between belief and behavior, and so he failed to fully experience his new life in Christ.

All of the people I've mentioned felt a split within themselves. They may feel one way and think another, or choose one way and yet act another. The apostle Paul experienced this and cried out, "I do not understand what I do. For what I want to do I do not do, but what I hate I do. . . . What a wretched man I am!" (Rom 7:15, 23). How many times have you felt wretched like this? We often don't feel whole and yet don't seem to be able to find the handles to get ourselves back in control.

People who seem to have it all together are so distressing. That doesn't mean that I don't admire them; but they distress me because they seem to go through life so easily while others of us struggle. Foxie had undoubtedly seen other foxes who spent more time enjoying the forest and less time agonizing over the trees. True, not all people who appear to have it together actually do. However, that doesn't help much when I am at war with myself, pulled in several directions at once.

Lack of unity or consistency within can cause us to behave in strange ways. My colleague, Daryl, and I often talk about ways in which people sabotage themselves.

Jim is a good example. He aspires to be a leader. He loves recognition, and he loves the feelings he has gotten from rallying people behind a cause. Recently, though, each time Jim has been selected for a leadership position, he has either withdrawn or become physically ill. "What is his problem?" everyone wants to know. His problem is fear. He doesn't trust himself, and he is afraid to trust others to support him while he tries to develop his leadership skills. "I just can't let those people down," he cries. And yet he doesn't seem to realize that by withdrawing he is not only letting others down but is ruining his own chances for growth. The divisions within him are as solid as brick.

The Need for Wholeness

Jim and others like him have all the right pieces and yet cannot seem to make them work together. There is definitely a lack of unity within the self. Psychologists call this problem disequilibriation. The A and B and C of our selves just don't add up. We lack completeness. Scripture indicates that God wants us to be whole in three ways. First, we are to be completed by establishing a relationship with Christ. "For in Christ all the fullness of the Deity lives in bodily form, and you have been given fullness in Christ, who is the head over every power and authority" (Col 2:9-10).

Second, we find completeness in relating to other people. The church is God's way of offering us interpersonal wholeness.

God has arranged the parts in the body, every one of them, just as he wanted them to be. If they were all one part, where would the body be? As it is, there are many parts, but one body. The eye cannot say to the hand, "I don't need you!" And the head cannot say to the feet, "I don't need you!" . . . If one part suffers, every part suffers with it; if one part is honored, every part rejoices with it. Now you are the body of Christ, and each one of you is a part of it. (1 Cor 12:18-21, 26-27)

Third, completeness comes in an undivided self, in being at peace with yourself. Paul spoke to Timothy about this internal wholeness. "For God did not give us a spirit of timidity, but a spirit of power, of love and of self-discipline" (2 Tim 1:7). Our emotions, thoughts and actions are all to be united by the power of the Spirit of God within.

Yet if the power is there, why do we feel so weak? Why are our feelings about God so often confused? We yearn for union with God because our Creator originally made us for that purpose. But the Fall has thrust another force in our lives, creating an internal push-pull. Our hearts yearn for him and the unity he can bring, while at the same time we run from him, trying to find unity in ourselves alone.

Hindrances to Wholeness

What keeps us divided and in so much turmoil and pain? Most obvious is sin. When I refuse to live God's way, choosing disobedience, I am fracturing myself. I may experience pleasure, but I also experience guilt and confusion. When I sin I am being divided. I cannot be whole when I am denying God's care and influence in my life.

When Saul of Tarsus met Christ in a vision on the road to Damascus, God said to him, "You've been bucking my plans all along. Now I have other plans for your life." Saul's hindrance to wholeness, his personal sin, was forgiven, and he experienced God as an ally.

Wholeness can also be hindered by the sin of others. We do not live in vacuums. We affect each other both for good and bad. I may choose never to get drunk, and yet someone close to me may become the victim of a drunken driver. If such a thing were to happen, I would be shattered, robbed of wholeness by someone else's sin.

We know all too well from history and the daily newspaper just how inhumane humans can be. Even those who try to minimize the concept of sin are painfully aware that human beings are self-centered and mean. It is hard to live as a whole person when we are constantly being hurt by others.

Defects or accidents of birth can also hinder wholeness for many people. Many have trouble accepting themselves because they are disabled physically or mentally. The question, Why? is a haunting one. Jesus was once asked this question by his disciples. " 'Rabbi, who sinned, this man or his parents, that he was born blind?' 'Neither this man nor his parents sinned,' said Jesus, 'but this happened so that the work of God might be displayed in his life' " (Jn 9:2-3).

Disability, like death, is the result of the influence of sin in the world. Sin kills and maims. These verses suggest, however, that through such unfortunate circumstances God will show his work or reveal his strength and mercy. I have known many disabled people whose defects did not prevent them from experiencing wholeness and unity within themselves. I have learned from them that when there is an attitude of openness and an expectation of wholeness, God will provide. And, conversely, an attitude which shuts out God may be the greatest hindrance to wholeness.

Why Be Concerned about Wholeness?
When I was a young boy growing up on a farm in eastern Oregon, I had a strong desire to please my dad. One of the ways I wanted to prove myself was by showing him that I could work like a man. When we would put barley in the granary, I would get inside and scoop the grain to the corners or the far side so that the bin could be filled completely. After an hour or so my muscles would be aching, my lungs would be filled with dust, and I would be broken out with a rash from the barley dust.

One day Dad said, "Let me show you something." I stood by

him and watched as the barley went into the bin without my help. I began to realize that as it reached the top it would topple over into those corners which I had tried so hard to fill. Dad pointed out that we only needed to worry when it began to clog the auger which we used to lift the grain to the top. He said, "See, son, you don't have to get all tired and itchy." This was one of my first lessons in learning that you don't have to do everything the hard way to prove that you are a man.

I have learned a wholeness from my dad. His life is much easier than it is for most of us because he doesn't go off in two directions at once. He has learned to put it together. His faith works for him all week long. He is able to relate to people without fear. He stands up for what he believes, but he doesn't meddle in other people's business. He is ready to face life as well as death.

The challenge of his type of living has inspired me to write this book. My aim is to give practical help in living by faith in all aspects of life. Hebrews 11:6 states, "Without faith it is impossible to please God." If we are to handle the complexities of human existence and discover for ourselves what "to live is Christ" means (Phil 1:21), we must learn in a practical sense what exercising faith means.

This book is intended to help you achieve an internal equilibrium and a unity with God through faith. It is intended to help you understand the divisions within yourself so that you can break down the walls between them and function as a whole person. It is intended to help you deal with your itch, whether it is the itch like Foxie's or more like the one I got in the granary from the barley dust.

The next four chapters present some basic observations about what it means to be a person and what it means to be a person of faith. I especially focus on the problems of finding balance within ourselves and living consistently. Chapter five, "The Faith-Filled Life," gets down to the basics of what it means to trust God day to day. The last ten chapters deal with practical issues you will face in your daily journey: How does faith apply to your thoughts? How can you manage your emotions? What about anger, forgiveness, self-esteem, responsibility, choice and actions? Each can be a roadblock or a steppingstone to an undivided self.

2
Your Whole Self

"I AMAZE MYSELF SOMETIMES!" Sandy, my wife, said as I walked into our kitchen. "I think so many things and feel so many things, I don't know how it all fits into one person." Those who know Sandy would also say that they don't know how she does all the things she does. Some wonder if she ever takes time to rest because she is so involved with people. But they also come to know that she believes in making good choices for herself. She strives to actively be *herself* rather than just reaching to people all the time. She is also committed to letting her faith affect her whole person. She isn't always successful, but her attempts serve as an example for me. Sandy is, I believe, an example of what psychologists have called a congruent person. All aspects of her personality seem to fit together. It is this type of total person that we are seeking to understand in this book.

There is much confusion about the relationship between who we are and how we live. This is especially true when we add the element of faith to the already complex aspects of personality.

Belief and behavior. How do they relate? Faith affects every part of who we are: our thinking, feeling, choosing and doing. I have already mentioned Hebrews 11:6 which states that "without faith it is impossible to please God, because anyone who comes to him must believe that he exists and that he rewards those who earnestly seek him." This applies to each of the four aspects listed above. A main theme in this book is that when faith is applied to our total personality, it can become the unifying factor in life. Faith brings us back into a relationship with God. Through it God empowers us to live in harmony with him and within ourselves.

Faith is trusting God. It is acting on our belief that he exists and that he can be trusted day by day. "He rewards those who earnestly seek him."

We live in a skeptical age. Trust is uncommon. We are taught to take what others say with a grain of salt. We are applauded for being self-reliant. But we can't rely on ourselves because we are not always consistent. A friend put it succinctly: "I don't know which to follow—my head or my heart. How can I trust myself?" Lately people have tried to solve this dilemma by relying on sensation: "If it feels good, do it." "Thinking is good but feeling is better." "Grab all the gusto you can." Discipline and self-control, often considered hallmarks of the Christian faith, have given way to an emphasis on the subjective. Some Christians have reacted by saying, "Don't trust your feelings. Satan works through the emotions—shut them off." The dichotomy between thinking and feeling, mind vs. emotion, has taken on the prominence of the body vs. soul controversy that occupied theologians and philosophers of the first century.

Neither our inability to trust God nor our internal conflicts are new. With great agony Paul wrote, "I find this law at work:

When I want to do good, evil is right there with me. For in my inner being I delight in God's law; but I see another law at work in the members of my body, waging war against the law of my mind and making me a prisoner of the law of sin at work within my members" (Rom 7:21-23). This was a vital issue for Paul. But my optimistic nature leads me to point out that even in his agony Paul believed the solution was in his relationship with Christ. For he went on to write, "What a wretched man I am! Who will rescue me from this body of death? Thanks be to God—through Jesus Christ our Lord!" (Rom 7:24-25). Trying to understand how this works in our lives is a challenge.

Faith and the Total Self

Human personality is complex and often defies simple analysis or categorization. I have found it helpful, however, to consider four distinct and yet interrelated aspects of human experience: *thinking, feeling, choosing* and *doing*. There are many other ways to view personality, but I chose these four components because we easily recognize them in our daily experience. Figure 1 shows that each of these four components affects the others, both directly and indirectly. For example, thinking leads to doing. Sometimes this occurs with little consideration of how we feel or any awareness of our choices. I may think that it is time to go to bed and just go, with little awareness of anything else. At other times my thoughts

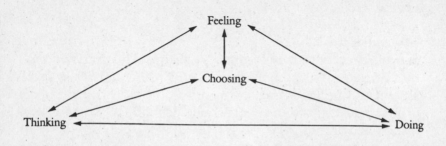

Figure 1   Four Components of Self

are modified by feelings and choices before I actually act (doing). I think that it is bedtime. But I am concerned about my uncompleted work. I still choose to go to bed. Thoughts, feelings and choices have all been involved in leading me to the action of going to bed.

The same thing can happen between feeling and doing. Sometimes we feel something and act without thinking thoroughly or actually choosing. I see a plate of cookies and impulsively pick one up and pop it into my mouth just because I feel like it. At other times feeling, thinking and choosing are synchronized and lead to integrated patterns of action. I am upset about the Bible study I am to lead. I could go and talk to my friend about it. I think about the time that would take and choose to study for the discussion instead.

Special problems arise when these components are not integrated. For example, our thinking about, say, extramarital sex may lead to one pattern of doing or choosing while our feelings may lead a different way. People hold to one view (extramarital sex is wrong) and verbalize those beliefs, but at times they follow their feelings to patterns of doing which contradict their verbal statements (they have an affair). This is what I call psychological dualism. Many moral issues often fall prey to this. Thoughts, feelings, choices and behavior may not come together on some of the most important areas of life. This is the time to ask, How does faith relate to each of these components and preserve us from dualism?

Doing Faith

Scripture records many examples of people who exercised faith by doing. "And what more shall I say? I do not have time to tell about Gideon, Barak, Samson, Jephthah, David, Samuel and the prophets, who through faith conquered kingdoms, administered justice, and gained what was promised; who shut the mouths of lions, quenched the fury of the flames, and escaped the edge of the sword; whose weakness was turned to strength; and who became powerful in battle and routed foreign armies" (Heb 11:32-34). The list of deeds is impressive. It is clear that God values faith that is demonstrated by trusting him in our doing. This is further emphasized in the book of James. James suggests that faith without works (doing) is dead (Jas 2:17). To do the right thing requires faith; to do the unfamiliar thing requires faith; to do the hard thing requires faith; to obey God requires faith. Lack of faith may prevent us from doing what God wants to bless. All these aspects of doing faith will affect us sooner or later. Actions speak louder than words, and it is our actions which give vitality to our faith. The reciprocal is also important. Faith gives meaning to actions, and it is our actions which give life to faith.

Failure to act out our faith leaves us vulnerable to human weakness and to circumstances. God seems to take pleasure in enabling us to do, especially when we seek his guidance in our choice of action. I have known many Christians who feel that as long as they are busy they must be living by faith. In fact they do so much that they often grow tired of the Christian life. When they grow tired, they sometimes feel that if they were just doing more for God they would be refreshed. Obviously they have misdiagnosed the problem. When we do because we feel we have to, our doing may not be of faith. When we keep doing out of dissatisfaction or fear, faith may be lost in the scurry for survival. When faith has been applied to doing, we do because we want to. Our actions provide opportunity for us to see the hand of God at work. As Paul wrote, "Whatever you do, whether in word or deed, do it all in the name of the Lord Jesus, giving thanks to God the Father through him" (Col 3:17).

To evaluate our doing faith, we can ask the following questions: Am I doing with a thankful heart, or am I doing out of a sense of obligation or fear?

When we take time to trust God, we find that the thankful feelings which are thus generated encourage us to trust him the next time we have something to do. In fact when our attitude is positive, we find new faith to energize our Christian lives. Faith while doing holds our various activities together so that they begin to make sense. It enables us to evaluate those activities so that we can weed out the ones we may be doing for the wrong reasons. Not all doing is good. Some of the things we do may in fact distract from the life of faith. The key seems to be balance—doing enough that we trust God in the process without doing so much that we become frantic. Sorting out this issue of balance requires that we look at the other aspects of our person at the same time.

Thinking Faith

Many Christians primarily apply faith to thinking. We place great emphasis on exercising faith in relation to propositional truth— sometimes referred to as "saving faith." "For it is by grace you have been saved, through faith" (Eph 2:8). 1 Corinthians 15:2 emphasizes that salvation comes through holding firm to the preached Word. Verses 3-8 specify the propositions to which faith must be applied: Christ died for our sins; he was buried; he was raised from the dead; he appeared to various people on several occasions.

We may argue that our faith is in a Person (Jesus Christ) and not in propositions about that Person, but many people never get beyond the proposition to the Person. Saving faith then involves trusting a Person because of things that we believe to be true about that Person. We accept certain things about Christ by faith, and then as we act on that we may find confirmation of our beliefs in the other areas. Doubts are bound to come. But we need not fear them. We can face them squarely, and take them seriously because we take thinking seriously. We need to use the mind God has given us. We need thinking faith in the practice of Christianity.

I want to underscore, however, difficulties which arise from a faulty view of God. People in a variety of problems often have a view of God which comes from distorting Scripture. God is the totality of his attributes. Overemphasis on one attribute, like justice or love, without understanding the balance among the other attributes, offers an inadequate understanding of who God is.

For example, many of my clients are controlled by a belief that God refuses to forgive sins and is perched above waiting to punish us when we step out of line. What a pity! They fail to enjoy the freedom that comes from knowing by faith that Christ was punished for our sins, and God does not take his death on our behalf lightly. We need to heed the word of caution which Guinness sounds: "For some reason or other a believer gets into his head such a wrong idea of God that it comes between him and his trusting God. Since he does not recognize what he is doing, he blames God rather than his faulty picture, little realizing that God is not like that at all. Unable to see God as he is, he cannot trust him as he should, and doubt is the result."[1]

Faith applied to thought is not a once-and-for-all process. The more we learn of God, the more we can trust him for further growth. Trusting God with our minds paves the way for opportunities to trust him in other areas.

Feeling Faith

Exercising faith in the area of feelings is foreign to most of us. We have been trained to believe that feelings are a part of our human dilemma over which we have no control. Therefore, when we are troubled by our feelings, we often withdraw from God and fail to explore the possibilities for applying our faith. I have often spent an entire day emotionally upset only to realize that evening that I had not asked God to quiet my feelings or even to help me understand them.

Feelings serve as vital signs, telling us when things are going well and alerting us when difficulties are imminent. In this role feelings are neutral. They, like our blood pressure or pulse, tell us what, not why. They are neither good nor bad. Jesus acknowledged the presence of emotions and indeed was an emotional person. He wept. He loved. He was angry. In the Garden of Gethsemane he was apprehensive.

Scripture seems to indicate that we are to acknowledge our

emotional state and then to make right choices about how we will react to our emotions. For example, we are told: "Be angry and sin not," "Fear not," "Love not the world," "Do not let your heart be troubled," "Love your neighbor as yourself," "Be content in whatever circumstance you find yourself" and so on. Each of these—anger, fear, love, anxiety and contentment—requires a response in the form of choice and action. This is how faith is applied to feeling.

Consider fear, for example. Isaiah 41:10 states, "So do not fear, for I am with you; do not be dismayed, for I am your God. I will strengthen you and help you; I will uphold you with my righteous right hand." The context of this verse indicates that the vital sign of the emotion of fear has sounded for Israel. First, we are told how we are to react to the emotion ("fear not"); and second, we are told why a positive response is possible ("for I am with you"). God's people were depressed and afraid. God challenged them to exercise faith in the midst of their feelings by choosing their response. When faith is not exercised with regard to feelings, they may control us rather than serve their purpose of alerting us to the need for appropriate attitudes and actions.

When the Jesus movement was at its peak among college-age people in the sixties and seventies, a train was commonly used to explain the relationship between faith and feeling. Fact was the engine, Faith was the coal car and Feelings were the caboose. Many thought the model implied that feelings only get in the way; therefore, we need to be ready and willing to unlatch the caboose to ensure the orderly progress of the rest of the train.

Many tried gallantly to unhook their feelings only to find out that it didn't work. Julie, a twenty-year-old, stated, "First I ignored my feelings; I prayed they would go away. I acted like they didn't exist only to find myself immobilized by them shortly after returning from a campus prayer meeting."

Swihart suggests that without feelings we cannot know ourselves adequately—nor can we know God adequately. He writes, "We can assume that God gives us feelings so we will be able to grasp, albeit finitely, something of who he is in an infinite and, thus to us, incomprehensible manner. All of the circumstances of life—being born, growing as a child and teen-ager, living as a single adult, being a parent, lover and loved, and even dying—constitute great learning experiences. The possession of feelings to enjoy and to cope with is another part of that education. We learn who God is. We learn who God has made us."[2]

Knowing this helps us realize that Julie's dilemma is predictable. God is not going to help us unhook from ourselves the part of us that he ingeniously created for the purpose of knowing him (and life) more intensely. His desire is that we come to understand our emotions so we can follow him more closely. We cannot quickly discharge our God-given opportunity and responsibility for our feelings.

Choosing Faith

The last area of faith and personality to be considered is that of choosing. Choice sets us apart as separate, unique individuals. We do not have a choice about choosing because, as Gilmore has suggested, "not making choices is not something a human being can choose to do."[3] By not choosing we are choosing to take what is left over.

When I was a vocational counselor some years ago, a client asked for help in choosing from among five jobs which had been offered her. We weighed each of the five alternatives carefully, both pro and con. She became more and more anxious and could not decide. One by one the jobs were given to other people who could choose until all the openings were filled. By trying not to choose, she was choosing not to work at any of the jobs. Her desire for God's perfect will for her, or her fear of not being perfect enough for any of the jobs, controlled her, and she made a nonchoice choice.

Faith applied to choosing says, "I will trust God to help me as I commit myself to one of the possibilities open to me. I cannot adequately predict the future, but I can trust God to help me live with the consequences of my choice."

Hebrews 11 gives us two prominent examples of faith working in choice. Abraham chose to obey God and go to the place of his inheritance "even though he did not know where he was going" (Heb 11:8). How was he able to do this? Hebrews 11:10 states, "For he was looking forward to the city with foundations, whose architect and builder is God." Moses also chose: "He chose to be mistreated along with the people of God rather than to enjoy the pleasures of sin for a short time." How was Moses able to make this choice? "He regarded disgrace for the sake of Christ as of greater value than the treasures of Egypt, . . . not fearing the king's anger; he persevered because he saw him who is invisible" (Heb 11:25-27).

Sometimes we only react to things rather than take the initiative in finding out how God wants to help us find solutions. God invites us to choose to eat at his banquet table, but too often we come in late and eat leftovers or garbage. We fail to choose because we are afraid of ourselves, our abilities or other people.

Recently I watched a healthy young man eating bread from the garbage can of a restaurant in Seattle. I do not know his circumstances, but I wondered why he chose to eat leftovers rather than respond to the help-wanted sign on the front door of the restaurant. Choosing faith takes the risk of being rejected. Maybe this young man was afraid he would be turned down for the job, or maybe he was running from a troubled family situation. Maybe he was running from God. The possibilities are endless.

Failure to exercise faith in choosing often arises from the irrational belief that it is easier to avoid than to face certain difficulties and responsibilities. Often we avoid choosing because we are afraid of failure. We tell ourselves that it will be easier tomorrow or next year.

Being able to choose is key to self-discipline. Choices which require faith invariably require giving up something or risking something. A choice to go to graduate school will require giving up some financial security and changing certain relationships. In choosing to identify myself as a Christian in my neighborhood I risk ridicule. Choosing to break off a relationship with a boyfriend or girlfriend costs some security. Joshua's challenge to the people of Israel, "Choose for yourselves this day whom you will serve" (Josh 24:15), was a choice of consequences. The choices we make are important. They affect our future. The best choices cause us to rely on God and are consistent with how we express our faith in our feeling, thinking and doing.

Opening the Door

For believers, faith serves as the catalyst for integrating thinking, feeling, choosing and doing into a unified being. My firm conviction and experience are that my Christian life is the most vital and exciting when I live each day trusting God for something: for power to do, for wisdom and character to make a right choice, for the ability to grasp what I can't understand, or for strength when my emotions are vulnerable. My experience bears out what the Bible clearly states: "Without faith it is impossible to please God" (Heb 11:6). To trust him means to rely on him for specific needs in each of the four areas.

Where does one begin to grasp the intricacies of living in Christ? We begin to see the relevance of Christ to our everyday problems when we begin to trust him for something specific. Trust is a necessity for living as a whole person. God thinks it is so important that we come to him voluntarily that he refuses to force himself on us. He only knocks. We have to open the door.

3
The
Balanced
Life

A FRIEND AND FELLOW FACULTY member at the University of Nebraska, Lincoln, used to drive me crazy with his optimism. Laughing, he would remind me of my tendency to view life negatively. "There are no problems," he would say, "just opportunities."

Although my friend had his own imbalance, he was quick to point out my overly pessimistic attitudes. It is possible to be negative to a fault, and it is also possible to be so positive that you are not accurately considering all the facts. Finding a balance is one of the key elements in developing a faith that holds together.

Imbalance is also possible in the four areas of thinking, feeling, choosing and doing. Joe is analytical. He spends all his time thinking, trying to figure things out. However, he is lonely. He isn't sensitive to people. They withdraw from him. His self-inflicted isolation causes him to make choices and do things which tend to increase the isolation. To prove his worth he freely uses analytical thinking. But that makes him appear harsh and uncaring. His life lacks balance.

Susie, a college sophomore, prides herself on being in touch with people. She spends hours with others laughing, crying, talking and listening. She wants desperately to be understood and accepted by others. However, she isn't very discerning. Both girlfriends and boyfriends constantly take advantage of her. She lives a reactive life. Because she is afraid of what others might think, she has problems making decisions and taking action. She isn't doing well in school. Her spiritual life is suffering from her failure to take the initiative to get solid teaching that will challenge her mind. She is out of balance.

Tom is twenty-eight years old and has been a practicing attorney for four years. His whole life is wrapped up in his job. He is constantly going, going, going. He was a shattered man when he came to see me last week. His college sweetheart, now his wife, had just asked for a divorce. "You never spend time with me," she said. "I don't know who you are." Tom is not unusual. Many of us have to be crushed emotionally before we face the imbalances in our lives.

Dr. Gordon McMinn has said, "The human experience is a process of learning balance. Healthy growth requires an understanding of the components of our make-up, and the ability to develop each component proportionately to maintain balance. If one part of us grows rapidly while the other components are not growing at all, then balance is destroyed. The human experience is less than it could be, for we are growing at a 'tilt' rather than evenly."[1]

Learning Channels
We need to look carefully at the interaction of thinking, feeling, doing and choosing to better understand the need for balance.

Obviously, we do not all approach life with the same strengths. Some people are strong in doing, some in choosing, some in thinking and some in feeling. We must come to know our strengths and weaknesses in these four areas, maximizing our strong area while strengthening the other three. If you don't know your feelings, find someone who does and learn from that person. If you can't make decisions, find someone who is strong in choosing. If you are afraid to do things, take the risk even though you feel awkward at first. If your thinking is weak, exercise your mind! Reading and study groups can be invaluable resources for this.

Dr. Paul Welter refers to the various aspects of our person as learning channels.

One way to understand the concept of learning channels is to imagine that you live in a TV viewing area where you are able to get three channels, only one of which gives you good reception. A second channel is fair, although the fidelity may be poor and it may have some "snow." Let's suppose that the third channel is very weak. You have to work hard just to get the main idea of a given program on that channel. This is somewhat like learning channels, because often one may be strong and another weak.[2]

Choice is central to the entire process. That is, we make choices about what to think, what to feel and what to do. We can also choose to emphasize either thought, feeling or doing. These choices are affected both by who we are and by our experiences. Doing allows us to stockpile experiences. Feeling is our immediate analysis of the experiences. Thinking allows us to understand or explain our experiences. Choosing is based on all of these.

Living a balanced life is determined by the interactions among the four areas. For example, a choice to marry is affected by both thoughts and feelings. Sometimes a person may not marry (doing) because either the thoughts or the feelings do not confirm the choice. The person struggles, "I will marry; I can't marry."

Unfortunately action taken when feelings and thinking are not congruent may lead to dissatisfaction and regrets.

Mary was a college junior when she met Bryon. They were attracted to each other physically and intellectually, and their thinking directed them toward marriage. The balance tipped in the positive direction. However, the feelings were not so positive. At times they both felt good about each other and about marriage. At other times they brought out the worst feelings in each other. As the wedding date approached, Bryon began to feel more and more uncomfortable. He wanted to back out but, his thinking was affected by pressure from others, so he told himself that he loved Mary too much to call off the marriage. The relationship lasted less than two years before Bryon had a nervous breakdown. He should have listened to his feelings. Their imbalance could have provided the clue that something was wrong.

The relationship between Dave and May also illustrates the need for congruence between feeling and thinking. The two hit it off quickly. They were attracted to each other emotionally, physically, intellectually and spiritually. Everyone said they were a perfect match.

As their dating continued, however, May began to be bothered by some differences. Sometimes Dave seemed cold toward spiritual things, and he would push beyond the limits they had agreed on for their physical relationship. At times May wondered whether or not she and Dave actually shared the same values. But when they were together these thoughts seemed to vanish. She felt so good when she was with him.

May tried to talk to her mother about her uncertainties, but her mother was at that point even more excited than May about her marriage to Dave. "You are just getting cold feet," her mother told her. "I remember I felt the same way before your father and I were married." Unfortunately, May's feelings weren't causing her doubts. Her thinking was. But she went against her better judgment and married Dave. The marriage didn't work. The balance was missing that could have spared Dave and May from the anguish of divorce.

Their unhappiness might have been avoided if May had been supported in her search for harmony between thinking and feeling. Although we can never expect perfect congruence among the four aspects of our person, we should be cautious when there is a serious conflict. Some dissonance may be the result of temporary stress or difficulties which can be solved. In any event it is advisable to move slowly until balance is restored.

If you are trying to help people who are out of balance, do not try to explain away a conflict. Help them to struggle with it until they understand what it may mean.

Major decisions such as marriage or choice of a career call for balance before action. There are, however, other aspects of life where balance is affected by lack of information in any one of the feeling, thinking, doing or choosing areas. This is best illustrated by the way we get involved in new activities. One day in 1969 I came home from work at the university and asked Sandy, my wife, "How would you like to go to Iran for a year?" Her initial response was, "Fine! Where is it?" At this point she had positive feelings about adventure and travel, but limited experience (doing) and thinking about Iran. She was willing to try living in Iran for a year. As she began to read she strengthened the thinking channel, but the feeling channel grew less positive. As with most new experiences, she became apprehensive just prior to departure.

Doing something new leads to either confirmation or disconfirmation of our feelings and provides new information for thinking. "Try it; you'll like it!" suggests the need for going beyond initial apprehension to collect new data on which feelings and thoughts can be established. If I were to ask Sandy today if she wanted to go back to Iran for a year, her decision would be based on feelings of our experience, more informed thinking and an evaluation of the events that have taken place since we returned home.

Balance is affected by the way thinking, feeling, choosing and doing relate to each other and by the way we perceive these relationships. Since people have different approaches to life or learning channels, we now ask, Are there specific ways to attain greater balance in our lives?

Steps toward Balance

The first step is to slow down. Give yourself time to think, to feel, to do and to choose. Although you may be a person whose work requires you to make decisions rapidly, in general you will find that personal decisions may turn out better when they are made more deliberately. Balance is rarely achieved on a treadmill going full speed.

Dan came to see me because he was becoming bored and dissatisfied with his life. He realized after hearing a lecture on depression in his psychology class that he had some of the symptoms. When I asked him to tell me about his life, I was amazed by all the things he was doing. He was carrying eighteen hours of classes, working, participating in three organizations on campus and struggling to maintain contact with his high-school sweetheart back home.

"Dan," I asked, "what would you like your life to be?"

He responded with a look of amazement. "I don't know," he said. "I haven't given it much thought. I'm not sure what I think or feel about anything."

Dan, like many college students, was going so fast that he felt out of control. All the activities which he himself had chosen did not satisfy. He could not enjoy his friends, his studies or his work because there was no time to savor any of it. He was like an off-balance top spinning wildly. He needed time to slow down and get in touch with himself.

The Bible presents a beautiful picture of a cure for the type of problem Dan's life illustrates. After Mary had given birth to Jesus, Luke 2:19 tells us, "Mary treasured up all these things and pondered them in her heart." Getting in touch with feelings takes time. Thinking about our circumstances takes time. Evaluating our behavior takes time. Making decisions takes time. Here are some questions which may help you in this: Do I like what I am doing? Am I spending time with the people I enjoy? Do I have a plan for my life, a goal to aim for? Am I doing things I believe in? Do I have the grit to change what I don't like?

A second step toward balance is avoiding the trap of being controlled by power struggles or doing things out of spite. Many people don't do what they want because someone else has suggested it. We reject the idea to show our independence, even though we think it's a good one. We first learn this bad habit when we are preschoolers. By nature we say no to what other people try to force on us because we don't want to be controlled. When we look at ourselves honestly, we will discover that many of the things others want us to do are things we would choose if the other person were not there. "You can't make me do that" may lead to "I can't do it even if I want to because I might feel like you are controlling me." A power struggle usually indicates an imbalance, usually the feeling area being too strong. This leads to a tremendous expenditure of emotional energy with little payoff.

Here are some questions you may ask yourself to correct such an imbalance.

1. What choices have I made that have resulted in this struggle?
2. What are some other choices I could make?
3. What am I telling myself about this situation which may not be true (such as, I have to win)?
4. What facts are there about the situation which I am not considering?
5. What is my primary emotion about the situation?
6. What would I rather be feeling?
7. What do I really want to do?
8. What changes should I make right now?

Answering one or more of these questions and acting on your answer may restore your personal balance and restore the relationship between you and the other person.

A third factor in achieving balance is recognizing and controlling stressful situations. Knowing that life is not always the way you would like it to be doesn't make living easy. When I first met Sarah, she had not slept restfully for days. She looked so haggard that her natural beauty was overshadowed. School was not easy for Sarah, and her professors just kept piling on the work. Once she got behind, it seemed there was no hope. Sarah tried to cope by taking pills. She took uppers to stay awake and downers to sleep. By the time I saw her, she was so ineffective that she reported studying (sitting with her book in hand trying to read) for three hours and reading only a single page. Sarah was in trouble emotionally and physically because her natural resistance was low. How might she have avoided this situation? How might she have controlled her level of stress?

First, Sarah could have been more realistic about her goals and abilities. When she became overloaded she tried to drive herself rather than realize that she could reach her goals if she paced herself better. Her fear of failure became so strong that her fears began to pave the way to a self-fulfilling prophecy.

Second, Sarah needed to be less concerned about what others might think and instead decide for herself what was best during this stressful period of time. Nothing that others may think is as bad as the problems we create by letting fear control our decisions. There is a place for taking responsibility for yourself and doing what is best for you even if it doesn't meet with the approval of those around you. Paul Hauck writes, "Not taking control of your own life leads to endless conflict, neurosis, unhappiness, and, worst of all, psychological slavery. On the other hand, standing up for yourself can eliminate guilt, overcome fear, and make anger unnecessary. But it requires the most serious form of self-discipline—especially to acquire the quiet strength that makes others take notice without having to raise your voice or make a fist."[3]

Third, you must take care of your body to achieve balance when confronted by normal apprehensions. Sarah began to abuse her body, and in essence her best friend became her enemy. Her first step in recovering was to stop taking the pills and instead allow the God-given processes of sleep and relaxation to restore her ability to efficiently attack her reading assignments. Sarah's physical tiredness caused a distortion of her perceptions of how much work she had to do. With rest and help in setting priorities, she was able to accomplish almost everything she needed to do.

Minimizing, Catastrophizing

Another step in achieving balance is distinguishing between real and imagined problems. Some people rarely see and accept things as they really are. Imagined problems may be caused by exaggerating (catastrophizing) or minimizing the probable consequences of events. If someone frowns at them, they may think he hates them without asking themselves if perhaps the sun is shining in his eyes. If the rolls are slightly overdone, dinner is a total failure.

When dealing with a client who is fearful and losing control, I first ask what actually happened. On more than one occasion, by explaining the situation, the person realized that things were not as bad as they seemed.

People often do things that I do not like. Circumstances do not always turn out the way I would like them to. This is normal. Life is risky. On the other hand, what I tell myself about those people and circumstances is important in my efforts to lead a balanced life. When I begin to catastrophize, I don't tell myself the truth about the person or event. Such "awfulizing" distorts the truth about the happening.

My wife failed to meet me for lunch at the appointed place. Two true statements could be made about this situation: first, I did not like waiting, and second, I was worried that something might have happened to her. If my thoughts had stopped here, I would have been okay. But they didn't. My emotional signals told me that something was wrong. I became unbalanced and blew things out of proportion. I began to catastrophize: "She may be dead! What if she has had an accident?" As time went on, I became more emotional. "How could she do this to me? Doesn't she know I need to eat on time?" I jumped back and forth between disgust at being stood up and fear that something terrible had happened to her.

By the time she arrived thirty minutes late, I was hardly capable of enjoying the minutes we had left to spend together. As you might expect, we wasted time by arguing about some of my irrational thoughts.

Let me emphasize—catastrophized thoughts are rarely true. Instead of acknowledging that I dislike a class, I tell myself that I can't stand a semester with that boring professor. True, if I had my choice I would choose something different, but I do not have to let my normal apprehension turn into a nightmare of fear of failure or of exacerbated anger directed toward my professor.

Another way we distort reality which affects our acceptance of normal apprehension is called minimizing. Some people fail to see things realistically by denying negative aspects of their situation which really do need to be taken into account. John's reaction to his first semester in college illustrates the problem of minimizing. He breezed through his senior year in high school and received acceptance notices and scholarship offers from a number of universities. John didn't really have to work hard to get good grades. He had been coasting for three years.

When he received his first assignments he was worried for a few minutes, but then began to explain away his concern. "This won't be so bad," he told himself. "I know this stuff already. Besides, I can read faster than most of my classmates. The professor will have to slow down for them." When midterm rolled around, John realized that he should have listened to the earlier signals. They were telling him that adjustments needed to be made. Ignoring normal indicators of problems is just as dangerous as blowing those signals out of proportion.

Catastrophizing says, "It's horrible!" Minimizing says, "It will go away." Reality says, "This is the way it is." These three approaches to life are like three birds—the magpie, the ostrich and the owl. The magpie is constantly making a lot of noise every time a little disturbance occurs. He is the catastrophizer. The ostrich is the minimizer. He buries his head and fails to see things as they are. The owl is the symbol of thought and reality testing. What kind of a bird are you?

Go for It

The last step toward balance is striving for it. Deliberately make achieving balance a priority. It won't happen automatically. Ask yourself whether or not there is consistency among the four areas. Do the choices you make lead to the behavior that you feel is consistent with your beliefs? Are you being who you think you are? Do you have goals which promote steady development in all four areas, or are you just floating, waiting to see what happens?

Imbalance among thinking, feeling, doing and choosing is often seen in people who are suffering from an identity crisis. "I don't know who I am," Joe said to me. "I just bounce from here to there. One minute I'm up; the next I'm down." Joe seemed to be alternately controlled by his thoughts, feelings and his behavior. He was afraid to set any goals because immediately after setting goals he sabotaged them. He felt helpless in making choices because he seemed to choose one thing and then do another. He lacked a controlling principle to organize his life. As I talked with Joe, I realized that his problem wasn't that he didn't know who he was. His problem was that he could not take responsibility for all of who he was: good and bad, consistent and inconsistent.

Knowing who you are begins with admitting to yourself that you are your thoughts, feelings, choices and actions. Identity comes with beginning to weave these sometimes contradictory areas into a consistent pattern.

The book of Colossians provides a biblical model for doing this. We are to put off certain thoughts, behaviors and feelings. We are to put on others which are more consistent with the overall picture of who Christ wants us to be. Next we are to let the peace of Christ rule within and the Word of God reside within (see Col 3:5-16). These commands from Colossians thrust the area of choice to the center of the stage.

Growth and balance are the result of deciding. Not just one decision, but a big decision followed by a series of smaller though important decisions that keep us on course. A decision to send a man to the moon was an important big decision. Think of the millions of smaller decisions that were necessary to make it a reality! Many of these decisions were necessary because of miscalculations along the way which put the mission off course. The important thing is that the decisions were made and the mission was accomplished. Too often people get off course and then tell themselves that their mission should be to go to Mars or Jupiter. When that doesn't work out, they try for Pluto or Venus. Is there any wonder that we don't know who we are? Colossians 3:1-2 says, "Since, then, you have been raised with Christ, set your hearts on things above, where Christ is seated at the right hand of God. Set your minds on things above, not on earthly things." The verb tense in the Greek text is present imperative: "Continue to set your hearts on things above." We could say, "Be willing to set and reset your hearts on things above."

Knowing who you are results from evaluating those threads in your life that consistently appear. Balance begins with this step. Just to know that you are sometimes loving, sometimes angry, sometimes passive or sometimes aggressive isn't enough. We need to look at all four—thinking, feeling, doing, choosing—and strive for a blend. This is growth.

4
The
Undivided
Life

DEBBIE IS TWENTY-SEVEN, married to a seminary student and excited about having her first child. She is vibrant, vivacious and bright. Debbie is also depressed, withdrawn and hard to get along with. "At times," she says, "I push my husband's patience to the limits."

Debbie is not mentally ill, nor does she have a split personality. She is not even a carnal Christian. She is a spiritual Christian, but she also suffers from periods of grief and feelings of isolation from God.

Debbie is suffering from what I call psychological dualism. Her personality is not unified and therefore her behavior is inconsistent.

Dueling with Dualism

Ideally our thoughts and feelings come together so we can make choices and then engage in behavior (doing) that represents our total person. When choosing and doing represent our thinking and feeling, we are at peace with ourselves which leads to contentment and a sense of positive identity. This balance tells us who we are. Figure 2 illustrates this process.

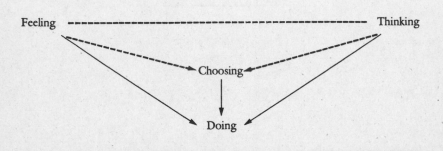

Figure 2 Psychological Unity

Unfortunately, this state may be the exception rather than the rule. What happens when our thoughts and feelings don't match? A consistent choice is impossible, and we end up with two or more sets of behaviors that seem totally foreign to each other. Debbie's life is an example of this. Comparing a psychological snapshot taken when she was vibrant with a snapshot taken when she was depressed, you would not believe that you were seeing the same person. Debbie's husband was frustrated. "She's the neatest person in the world," he said, "but when she is down I just don't know how to get close to her. Then I start acting strange."

Figure 3 illustrates what happens in one type of psychological dualism. Two incompatible sets of behaviors appear—one coming from feelings and the other from thinking.

This is not the only type of dualism that can occur. Sometimes feeling and doing do not converge to help unify our thinking. I must emphasize that although we are not as accustomed to choos-

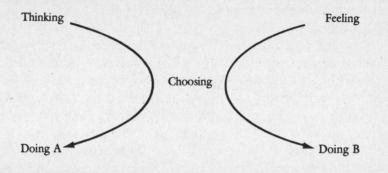

Figure 3   The Psychological Dualism of Inconsistent Behavior

ing our thoughts or feelings as we are to choosing our actions (doing), choice is still central to this process. Figure 4 shows how inconsistent thoughts can develop.

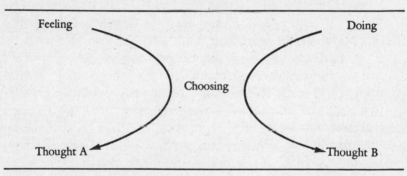

Figure 4   The Psychological Dualism of Inconsistent Thought

Jeff was a high-school junior. Garry, his Young Life leader, had not seen Jeff for several weeks but spotted him one day and stopped to talk. When Garry asked him how he was doing in his relation-ship with Jesus, Jeff surprised him by saying he no longer be-lieved in Jesus. They went to have a coke together, and Garry challenged Jeff by saying that he could not accept the notion that Jeff no longer believed in Jesus. Garry reminded Jeff of how ex-cited he had been after he received Christ.

"Are you now convinced intellectually that Jesus is not real?" he asked.

"I think both ways," Jeff replied. "You see, I'm living with a married man's wife, and when I'm there on weekends I don't think I believe in Jesus. When you force me to remember all the things that happened when I was going to Young Life, I believe."

Garry pushed Jeff to admit that his disbelief was more related to his moral inconsistency than to his intellectual doubts. Jeff had developed a second line of thought (disbelief) to try to accommodate the dualism that resulted from feeling one way about Jesus but behaving inconsistently with his beliefs. Jeff lacked the behavior which supports convictions, and from this grew the doubts about his faith.

Emphasizing the need for obedience (doing), Guinness writes:

Choice is one of the root ideas in the word *believe,* and this element of responsibility and commitment is the key to the "obedience of faith" which is the heart of Christian discipleship. Stress obedience apart from faith and you produce legalism. Stress faith apart from obedience and you produce cheap grace. For the person who becomes a Christian the moment of comprehension leads to one conclusion only—commitment. At that point the cost has been counted, a shoulder has been put to the yoke, a hand to the plough, and a contract for discipleship has been signed. The decision is irreversible. It is not faith going a second mile; it is faith making its first full step and there is no going back.[1]

Dualism of feelings is evident in several realms. In romance, dualism is symbolized by such statements as, "He loves me; he loves me not." When facing new situations, we feel both confident and at the same time afraid. In relationships we often feel love and hate for the same person depending on which aspect of the relationship we are on.

After graduation from the university Doreen became a teacher in a secondary school in the Midwest. She longed for male companionship and sought deep friendships with single men and women as well as families in her church. When Doreen first came to see me she was depressed and filled with self-hatred. She had grown up with a strong tradition of thinking. She knew what she believed and why she believed it. She held sound, traditional Christian views that sex was intended for marriage alone. But her life had been made more difficult by her strong need for acceptance and affection and by her physical attractiveness. She had matured physically at a young age and from the time she was eleven or twelve had been forced to deal with the pressures of sexual advances.

These pressures combined to develop inconsistent feelings in her. She became increasingly intolerant of her peers and their sexual attitudes and behaviors. At the same time she was becoming increasingly legalistic about her own behavior. As a result she defined sexual behavior as sexual intercourse only. By her definition, then, heavy petting and mutual masturbation were acceptable. Her feelings said, "I enjoy intimacy." As distorted as it seems, these feelings were supported by her legalistic thinking. ("As long as I don't have intercourse, it's O.K.")

On the other hand, Doreen's sexual behavior was taking its toll. She was unable to engage in heavy petting without feelings of guilt. She hated her body and blamed it for all her problems. The only way she could feel peaceful was to separate her beliefs and behavior in her mind. Her body became the symbol of all her behavior which was not in harmony with her beliefs. She struggled deeply with suicidal thoughts. This struggle is depicted in figure 5.

Doreen was utterly amazed when I asked her how long it had been since she had thanked God for her body. Her dualistic pattern was so ingrained that she could not fathom thanking God for the body that she considered the source of the problem.

The effects of this type of dualism are devastating. First, legalism creates intolerance for others while at the same time skirting the basic principles of Scripture. Second, doing based only on feeling results in severe damage to self-esteem which in Doreen's

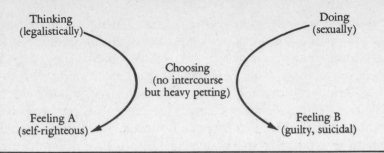

Figure 5   Psychological Dualism of Inconsistent Feelings

case was symbolized by her hatred of her body. She hated herself but did not seem able to stop doing the things which were fostering the hatred.

Inconsistent behavior, inconsistent thought and inconsistent feelings do not exhaust the possibility for dualism, but they amply reveal the inherent dangers. Let's look at the causes of dualism and then some suggestions to resolve this problem.

Causes of Dualism

An imbalance among feeling, thinking, choosing and doing predisposes us to psychological dualism. Though we may ignore one area, it will force its way into our lives. If we emphasize thinking and pay little attention to feelings, then the feelings may begin to take on greater prominence, making us behave in a nonintegrated way in an attempt to resolve the feelings. Thus, dualism begins.

The principle of equilibration is widely accepted in the social sciences. When we get out of balance, our system naturally does something to restore equilibrium. But often the corrective action is not integrated into our lives and dualism results.

Many children in their elementary school years are dominated by thinking, with the feeling, doing and choosing getting little exercise. This may work well during the early school years since it produces quasi-adult behavior that results in social compliance and consistent, although noncommitted, behavior. But later problems can develop.

46

John was a good student, a teacher's dream. He never caused his parents a moment of trouble. But John's parents wondered if there was something demonic about turning twelve because it was then that he began to change. His grades went to pot. He became belligerent and sassy. The close ties with his parents vanished. He said he believed in many of the same things as before, but his attitudes were different, and his behavior was inconsistent with his stated beliefs. He was constantly in trouble, and his parents were at the breaking point emotionally.

For John, this dualism was like a stage he went through as he sorted out his own values and became more autonomous. He matured into an integrated person. For countless others, the spiritual and psychological dualism remains and spreads to many aspects of their life. They struggle and never seem to find the balance they seek.

A second cause of dualism results from failure to resolve the normal struggles that result from the two natures within us. Hundreds of thousands of pages have been written to explain the battle between good and evil that wages within the human being. Paul, the apostle, said it so eloquently: "For I have the desire to do what is good, but I cannot carry it out. For what I do is not the good I want to do; no, the evil I do not want to do—this I keep on doing" (Rom 7:18-19). Struggling is part of being human. The way the struggle is resolved will determine the kind of person you become.

The key is acceptance. We must accept ourselves as struggling persons, and accept God as one who loves people—even when they struggle. Obedience, repentance and faith are the key elements that keep the normal struggles in life from deteriorating into a dualism that destroys us. Obedience says, "I want to want to please God. I won't always follow him perfectly, but that is my desire." Repentance says, "I want to see things as God sees them. When I fall by the wayside I will crawl back on the path. I will push forward and not remain on the sidelines." Faith says, "God cares about me and has my best interests at heart. I will trust him to bring together my thinking and feeling, choosing and doing. He will love and help me even when I feel more like a bandit than a brigadier general."

Phillip Swihart has pointed out the need to confess (admit to ourselves) feelings rather than express (act them out) or repress (deny) them.[2] Both inappropriate expression of feelings and repression of feelings may be present in instances of psychological dualism.

Dualism often results when parental or peer pressures force us to express inappropriate feelings. Such pressures can cause us to become obsessed with the need to please others. We may become rebellious. As the pressure mounts, our thoughts and behavior may become inconsistent. This is the dualism of the Sunday morning Christian. Such a person maintains behavior consistent with beliefs on Sunday, but during the rest of the week a contrary lifestyle dominates.

Repressing feelings can also result in dualism. Some people deny themselves to the point that the areas of denial become highly desirable. For example, the longing to smoke (doing) may become much stronger in the young man who is told that he may not smoke. As the desire to smoke arises, he becomes dualistic. He thinks smoking is wrong, but his feeling and doing don't match his thinking.

Melissa is afraid of horses, but she has never been able to talk to anyone about her fears because she has received so much praise for being confident around horses. Thus, she is drawn to horses because of the praise she has received, but at the same time she is repelled by fear. When Melissa admits her fears, then they can be dealt with honestly, and she can be helped to choose whether or not to overcome them.

Permanent dualism may result when significant people in our lives refuse to allow us to have fears and subsequently push us more deeply into the feared activity. I met Jim when I was a counselor in my first year at Idaho State University. We hit it off well because we were both new. Jim was a first-year student in the college of pharmacology. His father wasn't going to be satisfied with anything less than Jim's becoming the neighborhood pharmacist. Jim never told his dad how he hated chemistry or how afraid he was of competition in the classroom. One set of behaviors said, "I'm striving to please Dad." The other set of behaviors directly sabotaged his efforts as a student. He stayed out late at night drinking, which was also against his father's wishes. He withheld his assignments from the instructors even when he had finished them on time.

When we talked of his feelings, he realized that he was dealing with his fear of failure by making it happen. At least he could always tell himself that he could have made it if he had tried. What a waste of time, money and emotional energy! When Jim dealt with his suppressed feelings he was able to face his father and choose a vocation that was consistent with his interests and his abilities. This restored consistency to his life.

Distorted God

A fourth cause of dualism comes from a distorted picture of God. When you desire to please God but have a misconception of what he is like, your behavior may become disjointed. Many people grow up singing, "Jesus loves me, this I know," but by the time they are old enough to return his love, they cower in the corner because they have only a picture of a God who zaps. Where does the distortion come from?

We tend to fashion our image of God from other authority figures like parents or teachers. Difficulties arise when these people are harsh, inconsistent, or weak—all the things that God is not. Dualism arises as our thinking tells us that God is omnipresent, omnipotent and omniscient, and yet our own experience with authority figures tells us that God is distant, weak and doesn't always know what is best. We say that God is sovereign, but we feel and behave as though he can't be trusted with anything important. Patty, a twenty-seven-year-old business manager, said it clearly, "I believe in the sovereignty of God. I just don't trust him to meet my need for a relationship with a man. I manipulate those relationships and they don't last."

A distorted picture of God and the accompanying dualism may also result from creating God in your own image. I know myself better than I know anyone else and, therefore, begin to think, feel or act as though God were like me. When I'm not capable of loving, I project that image on him. When I'm inconsistent, I function under the misconception that he too must be like that. When I fail to meet my own standards, I tell myself that he has let me down. When this happens my thinking and feelings separate, and I make choices that result in two separate patterns of behavior.

Not exercising faith can create the same problem. Our knowledge of God, based on revelation in nature or the Bible, is often stopped at the thinking area. This awareness of God needs to be integrated into our feelings and behavior to avoid dualism.

Jonathan came to my office the first time because his hatred for his father had grown so much that he was planning how to kill him. This shocked Jonathan deeply. "What's a good Christian man like me doing thinking about murder?" he asked with tears streaming down his cheeks. As we talked, I gradually realized that Jonathan's difficulties in his relationship with his father were tied to distortions of God.

I started our next session with a simple request: "Tell me when you first realized that God loved you."

Jonathan lowered his eyes and sat motionless for a few moments, and then became restless. Finally, he looked up at me and said, "Why didn't you ask me to tell you when I received Christ as my Savior?"

"I don't doubt your salvation. I just want to know more about your love relationship with Jesus."

His head dropped again, and he said, "The answer to your question is never."

I sat quietly, respecting his sorrow, and then asked for eye contact. When he looked at me, I simply said, "We don't have anywhere to go but up, do we?"

With fearful anticipation he said, "I guess not."

A month later Jonathan went home to visit his parents. When he returned and came to see me, I knew something important had happened. "You won't believe it," he said. While he was helping his father with the farm chores, Jonathan got an urge to ask his dad some questions. The first one was, "Dad, when was the first time you really realized that God loved you?"

Jonathan was utterly amazed at his father's response: "Why didn't you ask me to tell you when I received Christ as my Savior?"

With tears streaming down his cheeks, Jonathan told me, "At that moment I no longer had a need to kill him. I realized he was as miserable as I was." Our conversation took an upbeat as we considered the possibility that God would use Jonathan to be the vehicle to teach his dad about God's love.

Jonathan knew all the answers, like "God is love." However, his distorted picture of God said, "God doesn't care about me at all. In fact he must be like my father who cuts me down and makes demands on me without ever showing me the support I desperately need." The spiritual and psychological dualism that resulted from a distorted picture of God had brought Jonathan to the brink of murder.

As human beings, we want to have all the answers. This desire was so strong in Adam and Eve that they disobeyed God and ate from the tree of the knowledge of good and evil. Their sin resulted in anxiety and fear of God. They hid themselves. From that time until now the human race has feared new experiences. We don't really want any surprises. Of course, this isn't living by faith. We strive more and more to have all the answers rather than to accept the dynamic relationship that God wants to have with us. We even absolutize the relatives. We try to tie up all the loose ends. My wife once said, "I don't know why, but I just have to box things up so that I don't have to deal with them. Maybe I feel more secure that way."

On the other hand, when it comes to obeying God, we ask ourselves, "Has God really said that? Surely he didn't mean it!" We rationalize Scripture to *allow* for our failure rather than admitting and confessing failures. This results in dualism in our spiritual lives which prevents growth. You never advance to meet God's standard when you lower that standard to the level of your stunted growth. Jesus' response to this type of dualism was usually quite simple: "Go and sin no more." He knows that you want to follow him, but he also realizes that you are tempted to move in two directions at once.

A final cause of dualism is working to meet our needs without God. The Bible calls this vain striving. Instead of manipulating truth or changing our view of God, we try to manipulate people. We have failed to exercise faith.

As the father of three teen-agers, I have been confronted with the fact that I try to live out many of my unfulfilled desires through my children. This is particularly true because of my lack of success in sports despite my competitive nature. I might as well say it: I'm a frustrated athlete. I forced my son to go out for cross-country; tactlessly I encouraged him in his wrestling and refused to let him slide out of track competition in the spring. At the district meet he ran his personal best time in the 1500 meters and qualified for the AAU meet. Imagine my letdown when he announced that he was going to go fishing instead of taking part in the meet! After an hour or so of discussion I passed it off by saying that he was just nervous and would get over it.

When I came back to him a week later he said, "Dad, you aren't going to con me into this one." I tried to make him feel guilty, but that failed too. He stuck to his guns and reminded me that he had done everything that he had promised me. I went away semi-defeated, only to return to him with a new slant. Each time I was rebuffed.

Finally, one day in desperation I asked him if he could be bought. He looked me right in the eye and said, "I don't think you have enough money." My wife was utterly amazed as she saw me come close to violating some of my own standards in an attempt to satisfy my own strong emotional need. This was dualism at its worst. I did, however, finally get hold of myself, and I wished him good luck on his fishing trip. I took the weekend off with Sandy, my wife, to recuperate some of my lost emotional energy. I'm sure my son shook his head and said, "Oh well, that's just my dad!"

We have seen how spiritual and psychological dualism may result from a lack of balance, from life's normal struggles, from failure to acknowledge feelings, from a distorted picture of God or truth, or from a manipulation of people or events instead of relaxing and trusting God. Each person is unique and the dualism you discover in yourself may be caused by any mixture of these problems or others. What can we do to find relief from the anguish that results from dualism?

In Search of a "Cure"

Although we've heard it so often that it seems oversimplified, it's still true that you can't solve a problem until you admit you've got one. Yet such a solution is anything but simple: It isn't any fun to look inside yourself and see the inconsistency or conflict which dualism causes. We may even develop the habit of ignoring rather than trying to deal with dualistic problems that occur. In these instances we tend to become withdrawn from others and even find it more difficult to get to know ourselves. But like self-examination for signs of cancer, looking at our real selves is essential if we want to be healthy.

The best cure for this problem is a good Christian friend who can look at us and tell it like it is. The challenge, however, is to be able to hear and receive whatever she or he has to say. I have been helped to grow by those who have had courage to say, "Earl, where is your faith here? How are you trusting God in this situation?" When I allow myself to hear and accept these comments, I am ready to take the next steps. But if I remain defensive and sealed off from the reality of my dualism, I will continue to live a life which is less than God intended for me.

A Time for Failure and a Time for Success

Another help is to seek a pattern of thinking, feeling, choosing and doing which will restore unity. Often the hardest question to ask is, "How do I want to live? I'm making choices which are contradictory. How can I choose so that both informed thinking and informed feeling are consistent and satisfied?"

To begin with I need to know the facts and to know myself so I can act responsibly in both domains. Then I can make an intelligent decision about how I want to be different (statement of the goal). Finally, I step forward and act on faith.

As we look at ourselves day by day (evaluation), we will find both successes and failures. We need to be ready to respond to both. I have found the following patterns most helpful in this.

When I succeed I will:

1. Praise God.
2. Acknowledge that God is equipping me.
3. Continue in the new pattern. Practice! Practice! Practice!
4. Praise God some more! It's delightful!
5. Look for new areas in which to apply the new behavior.
6. Pinpoint a new area of growth.
7. Start over with a new goal.

When I fail I will:

1. Ask for God's forgiveness.
2. Forgive myself.
3. Try to identify why the failure occurred.
4. Make corrections where necessary.
5. Praise God for new insights.
6. Start over with the same goal.

Too often when we are trying to grow, we allow either the initial failures or the initial successes to stop the process. If we fail, we say, "I can't do it. It's too hard." If we are successful, we say, "This is easy," and we forget that those patterns persist only when they have been practiced and practiced. God's work is not finished until the new responses have been thoroughly ingrained. This may take six months or even a year for these to become automatic. That's why we must pray for determination.

This is the key to success in any behavior change. Habits which result in dualism are strong. The beginning, of course, is to decide to trust God to help you change in this area. If you don't believe that he wants you to change, you are defeated before you start. God dislikes hypocrisy and inconsistency even more than you and I do, so you can count on his help. He will strengthen you and help you to keep on keeping on.

You will notice that the pattern suggested above is heavily loaded with reminders to pray or praise God. I have found that it is always easier to change when I have the encouragement of a friend. This heavy emphasis on prayer keeps my friendship with Jesus fresh and alive. Otherwise when I am successful I may become arrogant and forget him, or when I fail I may become discouraged or ashamed and withdraw from him.

When failure occurs, I must deal with that failure before I can proceed. I don't need to punish myself or to expect that God will punish me. I need to receive forgiveness from God, and then to forgive myself and move forward. Wasting hours and days flagellating myself for failure won't help. However, failure does demand some evaluation. Was there a specific reason why I failed? Were mistakes made that I can avoid next time? What can I do that might increase my chances of success next time?

I have often failed in my attempts to diet. In analyzing these failures, I have discovered something about myself. If I don't decide how much I'm going to eat before I'm around food, I will eat all I can get my hands on. If I am going to a friend's house where they usually serve snacks, I need to decide either not to eat or to eat just enough to be polite. If I don't make this decision before I leave home, I end up deciding by default to stuff myself. As you analyze your failure, be specific about some change or correction you can make, and then praise God for the insights and the opportunity to start over.

What about success? In time success breeds success! But! Only if you cultivate it! One of the reasons our Christian society is so weak is that we rely too heavily on quick cures and instant successes. In contrast, Jesus talked about counting the cost and disciplining ourselves as though we were preparing for a marathon race. When you are successful in thinking that desired thought, moving closer to the desired attitude, making a choice in the desired direction or doing what you want to do, take heart and rejoice. Praise God and acknowledge that he has enabled you to succeed. Then as you practice the new pattern, apply it to new areas. If you were decent to your roommate for a change, how about asking God to expand that to other people? The more a pattern is generalized to new people and situations, the stronger that pattern will become. As your growth in one area becomes more stable, add a second area to work on, but remember—don't neglect the first one. Like a tender plant, your new pattern needs to be cultivated.

One final caution about successful growth. Growing as a Christian can be like using a power tool. If I have to bore a hole through a log, I would need a sharp bit and power drill. I might try to do it by hand, but why should I when the power tool is available? I plug in the drill, position myself for action and press the switch. The bit goes cleanly into the wood and I feel successful. "This is great," I say to myself. My bit is really sharp. The shavings fly as the bit goes deeper and deeper into the wood. I reach over and pull the plug. "This bit is so sharp," I tell myself, "I don't need to use the electricity anymore. I'll just push this bit right through this timber." What more can I say? Without the power, even a sharp bit isn't very effective.

God Works and We Work
This introduces the next area of searching for cures: the need to cooperate with God in changing. Philippians 2:12-13 reads, "Continue to work out your salvation with fear and trembling, for it is God who works in you to will and to act according to his good purpose." You continue to work knowing that God never stops working. As you try to achieve greater balance in your life and

correct some of your dualistic patterns, you might become discouraged or even want to give up. "What is the use?" At this point you need to submit your will to God, and realize that successes are not accidents. They are the result of planning and perseverance. Maybe that's why Philippians 2:12, quoted above, stresses work . . . with fear and trembling. We work, although afraid and unsteady, sometimes even to the point of physical terror. The key, whether you are experiencing success or failure, is to stay hooked up with God. Philippians 1:6 tells us that he does not unhook from us: "He who began a good work in you will carry it on to completion until the day of Christ Jesus."

As a psychologist interested in learning and relearning theory, I am compelled to talk about the problem of trying to learn *not* to do or think or feel. The more you emphasize not doing, not thinking, not feeling or not choosing, the more those undesirables will be in your awareness and consequently the greater the problem of your doing, thinking, feeling or choosing precisely what you do not desire.

People who want to stop smoking and who try to do so by continually telling themselves that they have to stop, usually are not successful. Each time they tell themselves they must stop, the old desire is triggered, and so is the chain of behaviors which leads to lighting up and puffing away. A far better approach is to take away all the old cues and to work on the positive thoughts or behaviors you wish to instill in place of smoking. If a person usually smokes while drinking coffee, he is better off to substitute something else that is acceptable like, "When I drink my coffee, I'm going to call a friend," rather than to say, "I'm not going to smoke." Praying or praising God, for example, instead of thinking about not smoking, will not only help you quit smoking, but it will also be a great source of peace and joy to you, and a pleasure to God.

This process is especially effective if the replacement behaviors chosen are incompatible with the undesirable behaviors. For example, think about your wife's good qualities instead of griping about her weaknesses. This may even help you think positively about yourself.

Spiritual and psychological problems are rarely subject to quick cures. This is especially true of dualism that creeps into our lives only to become enthroned as self-defeating patterns. However, with God's help, change is possible. We must continually remind ourselves to become aware of such problems, to seek a pattern which will restore unity, to initiate a system or plan for change, and to cooperate with God in the change process. In all of this we should remember to emphasize the positive. We can become who God wants us to be.

5
The Faith-Filled Life

IN THE FIRST FOUR CHAPTERS I have provided one way of understanding psychological conflict and inconsistency. I have also highlighted some of the maladjustments which may occur as we try to live by faith. Not all trees grow straight and tall. Not all stories have happy endings. Often our lives become fragmented and our faith does not seem to hold us together. When we try to apply faith to our total selves, we must realize that we are going against our basic nature. Most people find that trusting anyone is difficult. Sin has undermined our basic capacity to trust. The reality of life is that many people are not trustworthy, and even those who are may fail us at times. Our dilemma is further complicated by the crushing realization that we ourselves are not trustworthy. We all grope in the darkness of distrust and are plagued by a sense of the unfairness and absurdity of life.

Learning to trust God is a sequential process. We learn to trust one step at a time. These steps may be large or small. Sometimes two steps forward and one step back seem to be the only way we can pick our way forward. Some of the steps to trusting God are thinking steps. Others are doing or feeling or choosing steps. Trusting God involves our total person.

A God Bigger Than Life

One of the first steps, as discussed in the last chapter, is to expand our view of God. We must put out of our minds the belief that he is no more trustworthy than other people or than ourselves. Trust is believing that someone is capable and willing to meet our needs. God is mighty and desires to help as we struggle to live by faith. Hebrews 4:14-16 emphasizes both the power and the compassion of Jesus our great high priest: "Therefore, since we have a great high priest who has gone through the heavens, Jesus the Son of God, let us hold firmly to the faith we profess. For we do not have a high priest who is unable to sympathize with our weaknesses, but we have one who has been tempted in every way, just as we are—yet was without sin. Let us then approach the throne of grace with confidence, so that we may receive mercy and find grace to help us in our time of need."

Constantly I must ask myself, "Am I allowing God to exercise his power in my life, or am I directing him by pressing him into a mold which doesn't fit? J. I. Packer in *Knowing God* quotes this warning of C. H. Spurgeon:

There is something exceedingly *improving to the mind* in a contemplation of the Divinity. It is a subject so vast, that all our thoughts are lost in its immensity; so deep, that our pride is drowned in its infinity. Other subjects we can compass and grapple with; in them we feel a kind of self-content, and go our way with the thought, "Behold, I am wise." But when we come to this master-science, finding that our plumbline cannot sound its depth, and that our eagle eye cannot see its height, we turn away with the thought that vain man would be wise, but he is like a wild ass's colt; and with solemn exclamation, "I am but of yesterday, and know nothing." No subject of contemplation will tend more to humble the mind, than thoughts of God.[1]

Part of understanding the bigness of God is realizing that he is both capable of providing the resources to meet our needs and wants to meet our needs. He wants to meet our needs when we trust him. He wants to bridge the gap between his power and our weakness. Many believe this intellectually (thinking). Few believe it emotionally.

As a senior in high school, I wrote an essay on God's direction in my life. My teacher's response was typical. On the last page of my paper she wrote, "Isn't it presumptuous of you to believe that God would take a personal interest in you?" At least I knew she got the point. I am presumptuous enough to believe that God is trustworthy. He is big enough and powerful enough and caring enough.

How do we expand our view of God? A key way is to read and meditate on the Bible. As Guinness has said, "God has revealed himself through his Spirit in his Word, and he continues to do so. Moreover, God is bigger to us than our small ideas of him and more gracious to us than our mean views of who he is. He is more eager and able to expand our faith than we are to have it done. We are all more shortsighted than we realize, so there is no one who need not count on the illuminating, mind-expanding power of the Holy Spirit."[2]

In addition to reading the Bible, read other books which emphasize the attributes of God. *Your God Is Too Small* by J. B. Phillips can be just the appetizer for the meatier diet of *Knowing God* by J. I. Packer.

Let me caution you. You won't have to read much until your intellectual belief about the bigness of God exceeds your emotional belief about him. Emotionally we learn slowly. But we don't need to become discouraged. If our thinking and choices and behaviors are consistent, our feelings will catch up.

A second way to grow in faith is to acknowledge God's power and trustworthiness in the lives of those close to us. We do not always identify with the way God showed his trustworthiness to the children of Israel; they seem so distant. But seeing his care for someone we know personally often makes an impact. Literally dozens of times I have heard my wife say to our friend Kay, "He has done it in my life, and he will do it in yours." This is why we are to meet together. We can encourage one another by sharing how God showed his trustworthiness to us on a daily and weekly basis. "Let us hold unswervingly to the hope we profess, for he who promised is faithful. And let us consider how we may spur one another on toward love and good deeds. Let us not give up meeting together, as some are in the habit of doing, but let us encourage one another—and all the more as you see the Day approaching" (Heb 10:23-25).

God is not trustworthy in the lives of people because of their spiritual maturity or great faith. He is trustworthy because he can't be anything else. That's who he is! God meets our needs even though we are different or feel inferior. This underscores just how trustworthy he really is.

Remembering to Remember

A third step in learning to trust God is to remind ourselves constantly of how trustworthy he has been to us in the past. Remember! Remember! Remember! How quickly we forget. When I was a child I always looked forward to family get-togethers. It was exciting to be with the aunts and uncles and cousins for a Saturday evening picnic. How vividly I remember, however, one Saturday when things didn't turn out right. Just before it was time to go, my dad sent me to the other side of our farm to close a gate in the pasture. As I hurried back to the house I saw the family car in the distance headed for my uncle's place without me. I was crushed.

I couldn't believe that my parents had done that to me. "I'll never trust them again," I thought. My emotions bounced back and forth between deep sorrow and extreme anger. I kicked the ground and threw rocks at the fence posts. I decided I had no choice but to run away from home. As I rummaged through the cupboard to find something to eat, my emotions erupted again. "They are eating all the good stuff," I said aloud with tears streaming down my cheeks. I found a few crackers and a little cheese, stuffed them into my pockets and began to walk up the hill away from home.

As I did so, my memory began to work. I remembered that my parents had always kept their word to me in the past. They had always been so good to me previously. I remembered that they had helped me get my work done so I could enjoy the picnic. I wondered what went wrong. The more I remembered about their trustworthiness in the past, the slower my steps away from home became. Finally I stopped, turned around and sat down by a rock.

I gazed across the valley toward my uncle's house and saw a cloud of dust coming in my direction. As the cloud got closer, I recognized the car. It was our car! I ran down the hill as fast as I could, put the crackers and cheese back and was waiting as my dad pulled up to the house. He was trustworthy. He had come back for me! All the negative thoughts I entertained were gone now. I knew he must have had a reason. When he told me he thought my cousin was going to pick me up, it all made sense. Dad wouldn't let me down. He never had before. He's not perfect, but he's my dad.

Jesus spoke to this point. "If you then, though you are evil, know how to give good gifts to your children, how much more will your Father in heaven give the Holy Spirit to those who ask him!" (Lk 11:13). Take time to list some of the ways that God has been trustworthy to you. Write them down and review your list often. This will help you expand your faith.

Redecorate or Remodel?
The first three steps to trusting God are specifically related to

thinking and feeling. Step four is a doing step. Begin to trust God in new ways. God is not just the God of the past. He is still alive and well today. What can I trust him for today?

Tim is eighteen years old and is doing well as he begins his second year at the university. Studies are no problem for him. But Tim feels inadequate around women. "I haven't even had one date. I don't even know how to talk to girls," he lamented. Does God care about Tim's love life? I'm presumptuous enough to believe that he does! God cares about all areas of our lives. However, if we want to learn this experientially, we have to begin to take some small steps to allow him to show us just how trustworthy he is.

In Tim's case, these steps were frightening. He had allowed his natural apprehension about women to develop into a full-blown fear. I told Tim that I could help him deal with some of his fears, but he would have to take some steps into the unknown if he was going to see God work. Taking those first steps is essential to living by faith. Being willing to try something new or to think some new thoughts feels like stepping into the darkness. Only when I do this do I realize that God is already there waiting to help me. As I open the door to the dark room I see light.

Tim began to step out by talking to the women he had natural contact with, those in the classes and organizations to which he belonged. As God aided him and he realized that he didn't die, he was enabled to take other steps like starting a conversation with a woman he didn't know.

When my cousin died, I was asked to speak at the memorial service. I am accustomed to public speaking, so this wasn't much of a problem. The feelings of fear and inadequacy came when I realized that I needed to go to the funeral home to view the body and to give comfort to the friends and relatives. How could I do this? I didn't even know how to handle his death myself. I remember trembling as I stared at the door to the viewing room. Sandy and I prayed together, and as we finished we realized there was nothing to do but to walk through that door. We shared the deep realization that if God didn't meet us inside, we would be totally at a loss. Symbolically, I gestured as if I were rolling up my sleeves, and we stepped into the room. Two hours and many hugs, tears and quiet assurances later we returned home, exhausted but peaceful because we knew God had once again demonstrated how trustworthy he is. He had met us in the space between our confidence and ability and the needs of our relatives.

But what about those times when things don't seem to have worked out as we had hoped? This is another difficult step in learning to trust God. Frequently we have ideas of what God *should* do for us if he is trustworthy. How often have you said, "I just want God's will for my life," only to turn around a day or so later and say, "I just don't understand how he could do that to me"? Believing in God's sovereignty intellectually is easier than believing in it emotionally.

Jeff had worked hard after college to get himself established in a job, a church and a new home. He felt good about himself and thought the only thing missing was a wife. He prayed about it and began spending time with a woman he admired and enjoyed. After some time he became confident that she was God's provision for him, so he worked up enough courage to ask her to marry him. You can imagine how shattered he was when she said no. As hard as he tried, Jeff could not figure out her rejection. All the signs had said that this was the one. He felt like a fool. He was angry at the girl, and he struggled with a strong feeling that God had let him down. He felt that he had trusted God all the way and had come up with a big fat zero.

Slowly Jeff began to rebuild. He needed to remember that God had always been trustworthy before and that he was meeting Jeff's needs in other areas right now. Jeff had to wrestle through his feelings of rejection and allow God and his friends to help him regain his confidence. The hardest part was realizing that the girl had the right to say no. Maybe she had the problem, not Jeff. Or maybe, just maybe, God had a better plan! We may have an interest in art or a desire to buy a painting. But this does not mean that we have the freedom to tell the Master Painter how to paint. God likes to hear our desires and is remarkably patient with our demands. Is it possible that he is just as trustworthy when he says no as when he says yes?

Too often in life we trust God for solutions to problems, but we only want the quick or easy solution. My wife sells real estate. Occasionally she has discovered an old house that can be purchased for little money down because it needs a lot of work. Some houses only need redecorating. This can be done quickly and inexpensively. Others have structural weaknesses or are designed poorly. These need remodeling. This remodeling may be time-consuming and quite costly. The buyer has to determine what the house needs to decide whether to buy the house.

Sometimes we need fixing up too. Usually we want God to redecorate us. The quickest and least costly method is usually the preferred one. However, the conflict comes when God, the Master Builder, recognizes that our needs are really for remodeling, not just paint and wallpaper. We may resist him and ask, "Why? Why can't you do it my way? Why do I have to go through all this pain? Why would you allow me to go through this if you really love me?" Intellectually, the answers may come simply. He remodels us because he wants us to be the best house we can be. Ephesians 2:10 says, "For we are God's workmanship, created in Christ Jesus to do good works, which God prepared in advance for us to do." As the products of God, we are in the process of being remodeled, as well as redecorated, so we can produce good works in others.

Savor the Savior

This next step in learning to trust God comes in the middle of this chapter because it is central to the whole process. We should savor God's faithfulness as we experience it. Often we plead with God and struggle to reach our goals but forget who helped us all along. To savor is to linger long enough to appreciate fully the experience. People in Western culture rarely savor anything. We gorge ourselves with food or drink and seldom taste it as it goes down. Similarly, we don't savor our relationships with friends because we are always looking for more. The Bible says, "Taste and see that the LORD is good" (Ps 34:8). In another place the psalmist wrote, "How sweet are your promises to my taste, sweeter than honey to my mouth!" (Ps 119:103). We only understand the sweetness of God when we take time to hold it in our mouths and taste it. This is worship.

We are so involved in the products of life—finding a mate, getting a degree, acquiring a job—that we fail to take time to observe the process God is using to get us to the product. If you are a tennis buff and a friend invites you to watch the Wimbledon finals, you would not be satisfied only to look at the scoreboard at the end of the first set. You would want to know how it happened. If you did watch the whole match, you would marvel at the skill and strategy that went into the winning effort. Likewise we should take time to observe God's action in our lives. When we do savor him we say, "God is trustworthy and he is enabling me." God must not be taken for granted. Savor the Savior! A delightful way to live.

As we grow in our ability to trust God, we will need to trust him in more difficult areas and in new ways. We are all different in this regard. Richard may find trusting God for money difficult while Gene finds this easy. But Richard may trust God for calmness while Gene is a nervous wreck. You may want to rank the four areas of thinking, feeling, choosing and doing according to the difficulty you have in trusting God.

Learning to trust God in the more difficult areas comes when we are willing to risk growing. Only if we want to grow, will we grow. However, we must stay at God's table for nourishment, walk in God's sunlight for vitality and courage, and follow God's exercise program to gain strength.

When my wife and I were first married, she was a relatively new Christian. She had spent the first three years of her Christian life in the greenhouse of a fundamental church and had gone from there to Multnomah School of the Bible. Sandy knew lots of answers, but she didn't know how to trust God. I remember how fearful she was about teaching a Sunday-school class. She believed that God could meet my needs and even her needs through me, but she didn't really know how to trust him for herself.

A number of years later she came to the table with our morning coffee and said, "It's okay with me if you die now." I was taken aback for a minute. I wondered what she had put in my cup besides coffee. Noting my concern she laughingly said, "I don't want you to die, but I have finally come to the place where the Lord and I can make it even if something happens to you." Eight years later we sat in a cafe in southeast Portland trying to decide how to divide our time as we shared the speaking for the Reed College Christian Fellowship. Sandy said, "The easiest thing would be for me to just let you do it by yourself, but I'm afraid to do that." As we continued to talk, I realized she was afraid *not* to put herself into the position where God could help her grow. She had grown from being afraid to teach a Sunday-school class to being willing to speak to the intellectual elite at Reed College!

Not only are we different in the areas we need to grow in, but we all grow in different ways. Examples are to encourage us, not to serve as absolute patterns. Taking gradually bigger steps of faith and having a more consistent willingness to walk while trusting God are the common touchstones of growth in Christ. We don't all have to learn how to speak in public, as Sandy did, to grow in faith. We are each unique.

The Thrill and the Agony

Another aspect of learning to trust God is sharing our victories and defeats with others. We can encourage each other by talking about God's faithfulness. We can also support one another when we fail.

There is, however, an inherent danger—comparing, either to elevate ourselves or minimize ourselves. Comparisons invariably lead to the sin of pride or to the sin of not exercising faith because of feelings of inferiority. Either way it is destructive. The Bible clearly states that we are to bear one another's burdens while at the same time we are to carry our own load without comparing (Gal 6:1-5).

Hebrews 12 indicates that we are to run the race, that is, live our Christian lives, with patience while looking to Jesus, the author and finisher of our faith. When we focus on Jesus we are not so likely to compare ourselves with others. Evaluate your conversations to see whether they bring the focus to Jesus or lead to comparisons with others. Even the apostles needed instruction here. After Jesus had reinstated Peter following his denial and had instructed Peter to follow him, Peter looked around and spotted John. "Lord, what about him?" he asked. Jesus' reply was rather curt. "If I want him to remain alive until I return, what is that to you?" (see Jn 21:15-23). My personal translation of this passage is, "Peter, mind your own business."

Another possible danger in sharing victories and defeats lies in the response we may get. It could be more of a hindrance than a help.

The book of Job offers a classic example. Job's friends were not as mature as he was, and their responses tended to emphasize quick solutions. Thus, they served to undermine rather than strengthen Job's faith. The phrase "Job's friends" is often used to describe responses to people which are well-intended but not helpful.

Do not give the responsibility for your life to others. If you need advice, ask for it. If you just need an opportunity to bounce your ideas off a friend, tell him or her that is what you need to do. Don't be bullied by well-meaning people who do not understand all the facts. Look for those who can help you to increase your own understanding and not just impose their view on you.

Beware of glib responses. How often have you had someone say to you, "You just need to trust God more"? The statement may be true but it isn't very helpful. Challenge your friend to help you to find some specific ways to trust God. Don't be intimidated by quick solutions. Falling into the trap of the glib statement will only engender false guilt which works against faith not for faith.

One further caution is in order. Keep a teachable spirit. Your friends may give helpful responses when you open up to them. Be willing to try out the things they say. Try on the shoe. If it fits, you have learned something valuable. If it doesn't fit, then you can look for solutions elsewhere.

It is difficult to trust God when you have been hurt by people. Just as God is bigger than our imperfections, he is also bigger than our friends' imperfections. Trusting him at such times is often the way God wants us to grow.

Jill was repeatedly criticized by Ruth because she wanted more of Jill's time. Jill felt overwhelmed. "I just need Ruth to care for me a little and to realize how frustrated I feel about time," Jill said. I encouraged her to confront Ruth with her feelings and to ask Ruth to look with her for some ways they could meet each other's needs.

Jill knew it was a risk because Ruth might not hear what she was trying to say. But she also saw this as an opportunity to trust God to bring about some healing in the relationship. Taking a stand was hard, but by the time it was finally worked through both Jill and Ruth had a better understanding of God's power to heal relationships.

Trusting God is a practical matter. Let me review the guidelines I have discussed in this chapter.

1. Expand your view of God.
2. Acknowledge God's work in those around you.
3. Remind yourself of God's past faithfulness.
4. Begin to trust God in new ways.
5. Savor God's faithfulness.
6. Share victories and defeats with others.

As you take these steps, let me suggest four pairs of do's and don'ts.

1. Don't waste time berating yourself for the times you didn't trust God in the past.

Do acknowledge past failures to God and agree to go forward.

2. Don't try to learn everything about trusting God in one big spiritual leap.

Do set small goals for yourself. Remember that the mouse ate the mountain of cheese one bite at a time.

3. Don't feel that you have to be more advanced in your walk of faith before you can receive God's love.

Do remember that God loves us while we struggle, not just after we have won the battle.

4. Don't give up when it gets rough.

Do keep your eyes focused on God and the goals you have set.

In the remaining chapters of this book we will look at the four areas of our personality in more detail. The theme will be how faith envelops each one. Let us begin with our thinking.

6
Thoughtful Faith

AS AN UNDERGRADUATE student in a philosophy class I was amazed to hear an unbelieving professor say, "Whichever position you take regarding evolution or creation, you have to take a leap of faith. You either have faith in an incredible set of circumstances which resulted in the beginnings of life, or you have faith in a God who could create life out of nothing." My professor encouraged us to weigh the evidence, but to remember that evidence alone would not answer the question.

His approach to education differed greatly from most modern methods which have placed a heavy emphasis upon the cognitive domain rather than the affective or feeling domain. Many people have therefore taken faith and thinking to be synonymous. I think something; therefore, I believe it. Thinking provides us with a more stable basis for faith, but thinking in and of itself will not create faith. Faith involves the whole person: thinking, feeling, choosing and doing.

In this chapter we will examine some of the ways in which faith and thinking need to be applied together to our relationship with God, our view of self and our interactions with others. The chapter concludes with how to control our thoughts.

The Base and the Faith
I asked Joe to tell me how he had come to know Christ. He acted a little nervous and then said, "I don't know. I just knew it was true."

My next question seemed obvious. "You just knew *what* was true?"

"You know," he said, "dying and all that stuff!"

"Joe," I said, "how do you know that is true? What if Jesus just died and stayed dead? Would that make any difference in your faith?"

As Joe and I talked, I became painfully aware that his "faith" was based on social support and pressure rather than any thoughtful consideration of the historical data regarding Christ which is contained in the Bible and other sources. Afterward I wondered if Joe's new faith was faith at all and, if it was, would it survive.

As I thought about Joe, my mind turned to my agnostic cousin. He could help Joe. He could give Joe the biblical basis for faith. He knows the answers. He can quote the verses. He just doesn't happen to believe yet! My mind had trouble putting these two together. How could Joe go glibly through life clinging to a Jesus he hardly knew while my cousin, who knows much about Jesus, refuses to accept what he knows. Perhaps Hebrews 4:2 offers the answer: "For we also have had the gospel preached to us, just as they did; but the message they heard was of no value to them, because those who heard did not combine it with faith."

Obviously, Joe needs help to think through the basis for his faith while my cousin needs to be challenged to apply faith to the basis. Knowledge alone does not please God. Faith applied to knowledge does. "Without faith it is impossible to please God, because anyone who comes to him must believe that he exists and that he rewards those who earnestly seek him" (Heb 11:6). Our thinking tells us why Christianity is true. God does not expect us to commit our lives to a faith which has no basis or to a Person who is hidden. God has revealed himself to us so we may know him. Stott writes, "The Christian doctrine of revelation, far from making the human mind unnecessary, actually makes it indispensable and assigns to it its proper place. God has revealed himself in *words* to *minds*. His revelation is a rational revelation to rational creatures. Our duty is to receive his message, to submit to it, to seek to understand it and to relate it to the world in which we live."[1]

I have always been impressed with the approach that Peter took to preaching the gospel:

> Then Peter, filled with the Holy Spirit, said to them: "Rulers and elders of the people! If we are being called to account today for an act of kindness shown to a cripple and are asked how he was healed, then know this, you and everyone else in Israel: It is by the name of Jesus Christ of Nazareth, whom you crucified but whom God raised from the dead, that this man stands before you completely healed. He is 'the stone you builders rejected, which has become the capstone.' Salvation is found in no one else, for there is no other name under heaven given to men by which we must be saved." (Acts 4:8-12).

In this passage Peter started with an observable act—the healing of the crippled beggar—and then logically explained the relationship between this healing and another knowable fact, the resurrection of Christ from the dead. The case for faith rests with who Jesus was and what he did. His resurrection from the dead, as historically recorded, provides us with a basis for affirming that he was the One sent to make possible our knowing God.

Dealing with Doubt

Just as thinking and faith are combined so we can know God,

thinking and faith together enable us to counteract the doubts
that result from our imperfect awareness of him. In their book
Unhappy Secrets of the Christian Life, Yancey and Stafford raise the
intriguing question, "How do you keep believing in something
you can't see, touch, smell or prove?"[2] This is the question asked
by naturalism. We are deeply troubled by the fact that we cannot
know all there is to know and that we cannot be sure of all that we
do know.

Doubting is a part of our existence whether we are wrestling
with the laws of modern physics, the laws of human behavior
emerging from psychology or our awareness of who God is. We
cannot escape doubt but neither are we left at its mercy. Guinness
writes, "Faith may not always know, but it always wants to know
what it may. It cannot be sure of everything, but it will always be
as sure as it can be. Where it is not certain, it will always seek to
ascertain."[3]

Doubt is never a result of thinking only. As Guinness's *In Two
Minds* reveals, we doubt because of our thinking, feeling, choosing and doing. Thinking, however, provides us with a basis for
unraveling the doubts which we experience, regardless of their
origin.

There are two phrases in Scripture that underscore the importance of correct input for our thoughts. In John 20:31 we read,
"But these are written that you may believe. . . ." In 1 John 5:13
the emphasis is on knowing: "I write these things to you who
believe in the name of the Son of God so that you may know that
you have eternal life." We are strengthened against doubt when
we occupy our minds with thoughts of the greatness of God and
the specifics of His love and concern for us.

Earlier I mentioned my high-school teacher's response to the
paper I wrote expressing confidence in God's ability to direct my
life: "Isn't that presumptuous of you?" It was not. Presumption
implies a lack of basis for the position taken. Faith and thought
combine to bring confidence. If I were to meet her today, twenty-
five years later, I could affirm that I had not been presumptuous.

Faith is more than optimism. As Stott affirms, "Faith is a reasoning trust, a trust which reckons thoughtfully and confidently upon the trustworthiness of God."[4]

Finite Minds, Infinite God

To understand God is difficult. His ways are not our ways. His thoughts are not our thoughts. His limits are not our limits. Indeed the process of thinking about God requires abstract thinking. We must project from finite human experience to the infinite. We have trouble believing beyond ourselves. We fall into the error of "creating God in our image" instead of allowing him to expand our awareness of who he is and who we can be.

John the apostle wrote from his personal experience with Jesus Christ. He wrote about what he had seen, heard, looked at and touched (1 Jn 1:1). Our awareness of God is expanded as we think about these things and as we, by faith, extend John's experience to our own. Just as doubting Thomas was able to exclaim, "My Lord and my God!" (Jn 20:28) after he had touched Jesus' hands and side, we believe as we consider these eyewitness accounts. Notice Jesus' response to Thomas: "Then Jesus told him, 'Because you have seen me, you have believed; blessed are those who have not seen and yet have believed.' "

Thoughtful faith enables us to go beyond naturalism to supernaturalism. We transcend our experience. This is not a wild leap. We must transcend our experience even in the natural realm. I recently watched via television as Alberto Salazar broke the world record in the marathon. He ran over twenty-six miles at an average of less than five minutes per mile. This seems incomprehensible to one who struggles to run one mile in eight minutes. I believe it because my mind has been expanded by an awareness of who Alberto is and what he can do. Thoughtful faith expands our awareness of who God is and what he can do.

I am amazed at the number of intellectuals who seem to deny miracles simply because such an occurrence would be miraculous. Thoughtful faith reasons that God is not limited as we are.

Thus he can do things that we cannot even comprehend. Note the emphasis of Ephesians 3:20-21: "Now to him who is able to do immeasurably more than all we ask or imagine, according to his power that is at work within us, to him be glory."

Our expanded awareness of God becomes the basis for *life* beyond the *mere existence* of so many people. Is there any reason why we should accept a view of the world which is limited by the finiteness of human vision? Thoughtful faith opens us to an awareness of the glories beyond. The God of the galaxies is also the God who the book of Acts declares to be very close at hand: "God did this so that men would seek him and perhaps reach out for him and find him, though he is not far from each one of us. 'For in him we live and move and have our being.' As some of your own poets have said, 'We are his offspring' " (Acts 17:27-28).

I Am a Promise
The more faith and thought combine to expand my awareness of God, the greater is the possibility of understanding my own potential as a unique creation of God. In Psalm 139:14 David writes, "I praise you because I am fearfully and wonderfully made; your works are wonderful, I know that full well." This awareness of the work of the Infinite in the lives of the finite gives me courage to live by faith in a desolate world. I can be optimistic about me. God desires to do his work through me, even though it means extending me beyond my natural limitations to do so. When I grasp this truth by faith and choose to act upon it, life takes on meaning that goes far beyond the stock market or the results of midterm exams. The delightful words of the Gaither song are not children's fantasy; they are adult reality:
I am a promise.
I am a possibility.
I am a promise with a capital "P."
I am a great big bundle of potentiality.
And I am learning to hear God's voice,
and I am tryin' to make the right choice.

I'm a promise to be anything God wants me to be.*[5]
Our ability to think allows us to take the possibilities of life and extend them into reality. Thus we are capable of studying not only history but also the future. We live in the past, but we are also creatures of tomorrow. This timeless perspective can contribute to either mental health, if we focus on the positive possibilities, or mental illness, if we choose only to fear.

Faith in God also allows us to go beyond circumstances to possibilities. We can give ourselves "as living sacrifices, holy and pleasing to God" (Rom 12:1). We need not be afraid to offer ourselves to God, because he believes we have something to offer. This great partnership with God is emphasized in Ephesians 2:10: "We are God's workmanship, created in Christ Jesus to do good works, which God prepared in advance for us to do."

In understanding ourselves we need to remember, however, what someone has said, "The problem of living sacrifices is that they keep crawling off the altar." The potential for blessing is great if we choose to stay in the place of blessing.

Faith to Love
Thoughtful faith also applies to our relationships with others. It takes faith in a God who is more than human if we are to entrust ourselves to relationships which are all too human. We want to be like those we admire, and yet our souls cry for recognition as unique, valuable persons. The result is often disappointment or stress. The need for dependence on God and interdependence on each other creates tension. We want to be autonomous, so in our fallen state we have little tolerance for the shortcomings of others.

Thoughtful faith in God enables me to commit myself to my wife because I believe God is at work in her life. He cares about her and he cares about me. His commitment to her and to me enables us to come to a place of commitment to each other.

I believe love in the biblical sense is impossible without the foundation of a thoughtful faith in a loving God. 1 Corinthians 13:4-7 says, "Love is patient, love is kind. It does not envy, it does not boast, it is not proud. It is not rude, it is not self-seeking, it is not easily angered, it keeps no record of wrongs. Love does not delight in evil but rejoices with the truth. It always protects, always trusts, always hopes, always perseveres." Such love seems unrealistic apart from God's power. 1 John 3:16-18 emphasizes how God's love translates into love for others: "This is how we know what love is: Jesus Christ laid down his life for us. And we ought to lay down our lives for our brothers. If anyone has material possessions and sees his brother in need but has no pity on him, how can the love of God be in him? Dear children, let us not love with words or tongue but with actions and in truth."

We are not only to be tolerant of our brothers and sisters, but we are also to be willing to sacrifice ourselves for them. God's love liberates us from the stagnant boundaries of self and allows us to engulf others. This miracle of loving each other is the sign God uses to show the world that we are following him. In other words, God does not take our relationships with one another lightly, and he does not want us to take them lightly.

It takes faith, thoughtful faith, to apply Matthew 16:25, "For whoever wants to save his life will lose it, but whoever loses his life for me will find it." The Greek word for *lose* used here is *apollumi*, which means "destroy, die, lose, mar, perish." You only have to read the morning paper to realize that human relationships often result in tragedy. God, however, delights in turning death into life. I believe he calls us to risk our lives so we might experience him at work in ourselves and in others. As we see him in action we become more tolerant of others and grow because of the faith of our fellow travelers.

Stability

When Joe first came to see me at the counseling center he referred to himself as a flag on a flagpole. He was up one day and down the next. With a strained half-smile he said, "I guess I am a double-minded man; I seem to be unstable in all my ways." Joe's life was not close to what he imagined a believer's should be. As we talked, we discovered that he repeatedly vacillated about his belief in God, himself and the world. His unstable behavior was characterized by either contradictory thoughts or no thoughts at all.

As we sorted out his thoughts, he began to realize that many of his ups and downs were the result of acting on lies he was telling himself. "God couldn't love me," he would think. "I'm too bad." After days of struggling, Joe's dualism and confusion began to diminish. He more consistently told himself the truth in Scripture without replaying all his old tapes from the past. Soon he began to improve on self-control. He also began to trust God more consistently.

Both psychologists and theologians have helped us realize that stability and self-control come from stable thinking. John Stott has written, "Self-control is primarily mind-control. What we sow in our minds, we reap in our actions."[6]

Thinking about God's love in the midst of rejection or failure takes faith, a thoughtful faith that goes back to the Scriptures. We grow in stability when we are anchored in the great concepts of Scripture. Note Psalm 103:13-14: "As a father has compassion on his children, so the LORD has compassion on those who fear him; for he knows how we are formed, he remembers that we are dust." God's fatherly love is available whether or not we ever had a loving father. However, to possess this love takes faith. As we begin to act "as if" God loves us, we see that love in our lives. We step into the gap by faith, knowing from Scripture that God will be there. The result? Stability.

Capturing Enemy Soldiers

So far in this chapter I have discussed how thought and faith interrelate. One of the important threads has been that not all our thoughts are true. Even some thoughts which are supported by our feelings may be both false and harmful. We must be careful to not follow the motto: If it feels good, think it!

The apostle Paul made this amazing statement, "We demolish arguments and every pretension that sets itself up against the knowledge of God, and we take captive every thought to make it obedient to Christ" (2 Cor 10:4-5). There are two thrusts in these verses which relate directly to controlled thinking: demolishing arguments and pretensions, and taking thoughts captive. The first thrust emphasizes dismantling those thoughts which are not based on truth. Such arguments support our choices, feelings, behaviors or other thoughts but run contrary to Scripture.

When my thinking becomes confused or I find myself building arguments in favor of feelings or actions which are contrary to my beliefs, these thoughts need to be torn down. If I do not dismantle them, the result will be the dualism discussed in chapter four. When I am in this frame of mind, I often need a friend who will challenge my arguments and clarify my thinking. I often call Daryl and ask, "Do you have time to do a sanity check for me?" I trust him because he won't just support my arguments but will make me evaluate them and see where they are taking me.

The second thrust of the passage is taking thoughts captive. There are some thoughts that are as dangerous as enemy soldiers. These stand ready to snuff out our lives if we do not take them seriously and deal with them ruthlessly. Thoughts of harming others, breaking the law or committing suicide all deserve such treatment.

Other enemies which must be captured are thoughts which indulge our doubts or give us permission to engage in sinful behaviors. These enemy soldiers may kill more slowly, but they do kill.

When taking a soldier captive, we identify him, confront him, control him, disarm him and imprison him. Lastly we leave him. Once the captive is locked up, we do not toy with him or entertain him. We do not take him in and out of the cell, or talk with him about whether he would really harm us if given a chance. War is serious business, and so is the war that often rages in our thoughts.

There are some practical steps which we can take to control

thoughts. We will examine these by following the pattern which I suggested for capturing enemy soldiers.

1. *Identifying enemy thoughts.*
In times of battle people wear uniforms. You can usually tell at a glance whose side someone is on. Unfortunately this is not true of enemy thoughts. They are usually carefully camouflaged, staying hidden until they are about to attack.

Such is Satan's strategy. "And no wonder, for Satan himself masquerades as an angel of light" (2 Cor 11:14). Much of Satan's masquerade is played out in our thoughts. Our thoughts dictate who we become. If Satan is allowed to sneak up on us here, he will control us rather than be controlled.

How do we identify such a subtle enemy? Here are some questions we can ask.
☐ Is this thought consistent with Scripture?
☐ Is this thought consistent with my view of who God wants me to be?
☐ Is this thought consistent with other beliefs and feelings I have?
☐ If I allow this thought to control future choices, will those choices strengthen or weaken my character?
☐ Does this thought support a Christian world view?

2. *Confronting enemy thoughts.*
Sandy, my wife, has often stated that she is not worried about me lying to her, but she sometimes fears that I may lie to myself. As I have thought about that, I realize that she is right. My capacity for self-deceit is great. I am vulnerable to fooling myself by entertaining enemy thoughts.

The only way I know to deal with this is to be ruthless with myself. I have to be able to say, "You are kidding yourself," Or, "You are playing with fire and you know it," or, "Where will this line of thinking lead you?" Telling myself the truth about the incorrect thinking is the hardest step. This is true whether the thought is related to personal behavior, my choice of priorities, procrastination or my view of God's power. All of these thoughts need to be confronted. Meditation on Scripture is so important because it forces us to slow down and to take an honest look at ourselves and our thoughts.

3. *Controlling enemy thoughts.*
Controlling undesirable thoughts begins with a choice. You choose not to indulge those thoughts which lead you away from who you want to be. There are two keys. The first is to stop the thought when it occurs and the second is to replace the thought with a constructive one.

Suppose you fear failing a biology class. The enemy thought is, "I can't possibly pass this class; I just don't understand it." It can invade your mind dozens of times an hour. When it does, you have to be tough enough to yell "stop" at yourself.

Some use an internal monolog: "Stop it! You are just making yourself more afraid. You don't know that you won't pass." Then new thoughts are forcibly substituted: "I can study even though I am fearful. This class gives me something I can trust God for. I'll do the best I can and worry about the consequences when I find out what they are. The worst that can happen probably happened already when I became so fearful."

To control our thinking we have to get down to reality. We must deal with what *is* instead of exaggerations. We will not die if we fail a biology test. We may be disappointed, and it may cause us difficulty. But we can go on from there.

This is where substituting the positive thoughts becomes so important. We can think about what we can do to make a difference rather than focusing on our fear.

Use the one-two punch. Stop the negative thought; use the positive thought of telling yourself what you can do.

4. *Disarming enemy thoughts.*
After you have controlled the undesirable thoughts and have

won the battle, it is helpful to relive the victory. Rehearse what God enabled you to do, and remind yourself that he will enable you in the future. This strengthening of the positive thoughts will serve to disarm the negative ones in the future. Philippians 4:8 presents the pattern for emphasizing the positive. "Finally, brothers, whatever is true, whatever is noble, whatever is right, whatever is pure, whatever is lovely, whatever is admirable—if anything is excellent or praiseworthy—think about such things."

I have found that most people have trained themselves to dwell on the negative rather than the positive. In fact one person said, "If I hear ten positive statements and one negative one, I will end up thinking about the negative one." The only way I know to disarm the negative is to concentrate on the positive statements. We don't have time for both.

5. *Imprisoning enemy thoughts.*
Focusing on positive thoughts not only disarms undesirable thoughts but also tends to tie up enemy thoughts. Each time we emphasize the truth, we wrap another rope around the enemy thought. Be deliberate in efforts to secure it. Enemy thoughts will often struggle when they are being tied up, but we need to remain firm. Obedience to God and faith in his ability to enable us to secure the enemy are the keys.

If these steps are difficult for you, ask for the support of a Christian friend. It isn't important that you be able to tie up the enemy by yourself; it is just important that you do it. Don't be so proud that you let the enemy loose just because you didn't ask for help.

6. *Leaving enemy thoughts.*
Once the enemy is secured, it is time to get out of the situation. Don't toy with trouble. Get on with life, and don't look back. There will be new battles to fight, so don't hold on to the old ones any longer. If they recur in the old form or a new form, take courage from your past success and go through the process again. Each time you do this you will develop more confidence in God

and more confidence in yourself.

A certain mental toughness develops when you are willing to apply faith to your thoughts. Just as it takes faith to follow the right thoughts in the first place, it takes faith to control your thinking and to move forward to new areas.

One new area might be that of your emotions. The next chapters deal with this.

7
Managing Emotional Investments

ONE NIGHT AS I SAT QUIETLY in my living room trying to read a book, I was not able to concentrate. My wandering mind began to think about money. Lots of money. Money for my children's college education. Money which I did not have. Just as I was approaching panic I was comforted by the sense that there was still time. "And I do have a few bonds," I told myself. I thought about those few bonds and began to laugh. I laughed because $1,200 doesn't even begin to pay for one year in college for one person, and we have five children.

As I sat there musing over the situation, I realized I wasn't doing a good job of managing the resources we had collected. Those bonds had been a fair investment at the time I bought them, but they were a poor investment now. Cashing in the bonds and reinvesting the money was a good experience for the children and me. We had time to talk about the investments they are going to have to make in their own college education.

Our financial investments are not the only important portfolio that must be managed. We also have emotional investments. I was near panic when I thought about the thousands of dollars needed for the children's education. If I had continued to invest myself in worry, other areas of my life would have been affected, including my relationships with my wife and children. As I waited impatiently, but calmly, for the bank cashier to redeem the bonds, I was aware that if I had continued to invest in worry I could have become rude to the cashier. Instead I chose to encourage her and show interest in her needs as a person under the stress of a demanding job. That was a good investment for me to make. Both of us were helped. I began to think of other emotional investments I have made, both good and bad.

Good emotional investments unify us as individuals. They build up both us and those around us. The best emotional investments are those in which we trust God to be with us and guide us whether in joy, sorrow, anger or disappointment. In other words we choose by faith to let God help us manage our lives.

Poor emotional investments result in imbalance and dualism. We fail to apply faith to our emotions. Our investment is not a particular emotion. It is what we do with the emotion. Feeling angry is common. Choosing to dwell on the anger, however, is a poor investment. In such a choice we fail to trust God. Distorted thoughts and undesirable behavior can result.

Positive emotions such as love can also be invested poorly. You may spend so much time feeling warm about someone that you rarely think about God or yourself. This imbalance leads away from rather than toward trusting God in your emotions.

We can make many possible investments. We can seek to be loved or seek to love. We can enjoy being angry or try to show patience. We can be content about the future or worry about what might happen.

We can also make poor emotional investments by spending our emotional energy trying to change the way people see us rather than just being ourselves. Precious emotional energy is lost when we invest in hiding from others rather than in being open. A client told me that he spent at least ninety per cent of his emotional energy trying to keep secret that he was homosexual. It is not surprising that he had little time to experience positive emotions.

Galatians 5, which talks about the fruit of the Holy Spirit, is really a chapter on emotional investment. The first three are emotions: love, joy and peace. They are freely available, but we have to invest in them. As believers we are preferred customers, but we have to allow God to pay the dividends. With tongue in cheek Paul says there is no law against these (Gal 5:23). Today we would say, "Go for it!" or in this context, "Invest in it!"

If you have ever been mentally or emotionally exhausted, you realize that you are a consumable resource. The most valuable resource we bring to our studies, our job, our marriage, our church can be used up. When this happens, we often get caught in the trap of blaming others for our bankruptcy rather than re-examining the way we are spending our emotional capital. We tell ourselves that we would be fine if the professors were just more reasonable with assignments or if the boss would just hire some decent help. We say that the children are at fault when we are wrung out or that our spouse has demanded so much we have nothing left to give. Blaming others may be easy, but it is never productive. In fact, blaming is a poor emotional investment itself. A more productive approach is to look within to discover some of the causes of emotional depletion.

Expecting Others to Make Me Happy

During our twenty-three years of marriage Sandy and I have been known to say to each other, sometimes loudly, sometimes muffled by a tear, "Why can't you just make me happy?" or "You make me angry!" Statements like these are poor emotional investments because they are subtly, but definitely, untrue. No one can make me happy, and no one can make me angry except me. People only do things I like or dislike. My response to their words or actions leads me to emotional gain or depletion.

I believe that Minirth and Meier are right when they say *happiness is a choice.*[1] Saying, "I don't like what you said, but I choose to believe that you didn't intend to hurt me," is much more productive. At other times I have to admit to God I am choosing to be angry. That is my sin, not the other person's.

Repressing Feelings

Repressing or suppressing feelings also depletes us emotionally. *Repression* is a psychological term from the psychoanalytic tradition that refers to feelings or thoughts actually being held back in our unconscious. This is a defense mechanism that the mind uses to try to help us maintain control or balance in life. Although we are usually unaware of repression, vast amounts of emotional energy will still be expended. Swihart writes:

> Repression comes at great cost for it saps our energies like a hidden short in an electrical system. It takes effort to keep these feelings hidden in the recesses of our unconscious. As a child, did you ever play with a bit of wood or a balloon, trying to push it under the surface of a tank of water? It was fun and fascinating because it was so difficult to keep it from floating to the surface. Keeping down feelings that we fear will blow up in our face or reveal us as some kind of monster is an energy drain that leaves us less able to help others and to be about the King's business in general.[2]

Repressed feelings will also have serious effects on our physical health. Nancy Anne Smith's personal testimony, *All I Need Is Love,* provides needed insight into unlocking repression and also suggests hope for the hurting.[3]

Suppression of feelings may not be as severe as repression, but it is much more common and just as devastating to our emotional resources. To suppress is to put out of awareness (usually temporarily) or to refuse to deal with a problem. Suppressing emotions is much like neglecting to clean a wound. If you let the wound go long enough, it may take care of itself or gangrene could set in. We tend to believe that it is better to put off dealing with feelings or issues that are fearsome. Procrastination with our emotions can cost as much emotionally as failure to properly invest my children's savings can cost financially. Investing energy in suppressing emotions is like investing in a bankrupt company.

When you keep a secret, you hope no one else finds out. But when you suppress feelings, you hope even you won't find out. Is it any wonder that so much energy is spent? The irrational belief that it is easier to avoid rather than to face life's difficulties and responsibilities is strong in all of us. The tremendous drain of emotional energy affects us all too.[4]

I function much better when I face a problem now. Putting off until tomorrow what I can't handle today seldom works. Tomorrow never comes. Or worse, it comes filled with problems generated by putting things off today. We think we are sparing ourselves by not dealing with issues only to find that these same issues have depleted us emotionally while we were looking the other way. Swihart has pointed out that confession of feelings is a far better alternative than repression or inappropriate expression.[5] If we keep up-to-date accounts with God and deal with problems in our emotions as they arise, we are invigorated at the start of a new day rather than drained.

I am not saying that we should never delay acting on our feelings. Sometimes we need time to evaluate what we are feeling to know better what course of action to take. At other times emotional stress may be so heavy that we cannot consider our feelings. In such instances supportive counseling may be necessary to help us deal with these feelings in the most productive way instead of suppressing them.

Guilt

Another poor emotional investment is guilt. As a Christian psychotherapist who primarily serves Christians, I find many clients wallowing in the guilt of past sins. They barely have strength enough to live, let alone trust God, because they are hung up on past failures. Unresolved guilt can quench the work of the Holy Spirit as thoroughly as anything. Anytime we spend more time considering sin, whether old or completely new, than we spend savoring Jesus, we are in danger of depleting our emotional energy. When we dwell on guilt, we deny what the Psalmist wrote: "As far as the east is from the west, so far has he removed our transgressions from us" (Ps 103:12).

Guilt is one of the prominent areas where Christians especially demonstrate psychological dualism. Most of us believe that Christ died for our sins and that because of his death we no longer have to pay the penalty for our own sins. This belief is based in our thinking and leads to the behavior of confessing sin and going on with living the Christian life. Emotionally, however, we see a different story. Many believe emotionally that God is the God who zaps and that he will not be satisfied until we have adequately paid for our sins. This dualism is nurtured by some of God's people who preach forgiveness while continuing to extract a pound of flesh from all who have done wrong. Failing to accept God's forgiveness leads to self-defeating behavior and an inability to trust God since "everyone knows you just can't trust people who are mad at you." Why do we still feel guilty when we know all that Christ has done for us? Bruce Narramore says,

> The answer is twofold. We still experience guilt because we have been trained to feel guilty when we fail; we also feel guilty because we have a deep desire to satisfy our guilty conscience on our own. In other words, sometimes we feel guilty because of the psychic remnants of our past. Our parents taught us to feel guilty because we are trying to solve our sin problems by ourselves. Guilt, you see, is essentially a self-inflicted punishment.[6]

Isaiah 6:7 suggests that forgiveness has two aspects: atonement for the sin and removal of the guilt. After the angel touched Isaiah's mouth with a burning coal, he said, "See, this has touched your lips; your guilt is taken away and your sin atoned for." Forgiveness is intended to extend all the way to the guilt.

In trying to solve this problem in my life I begin by acknowledging my sin, confessing it and praying for forgiveness. As I consider what I have done and its implications, I may find I have more to confess or I may, for a time, be overtaken with regret. This is a part of seeing my sin as God sees it. Eventually, however, I will come to realize that God wants me whole, not shattered. I must then praise him for *forgiveness received* just as vigorously as I prayed for forgiveness. I have realized that God is not through with my sin until he has restored me to the place where I accept his blessings once again. I cannot accept God's grace while I am drowning in guilt. In David's great psalm of confession and restoration he cries out, "Save me from bloodguilt, O God, the God who saves me, and my tongue will sing of your righteousness. O Lord, open my lips, and my mouth will declare your praise" (Ps 51:14-15).

Sound Emotional Investments

We have looked at three of the most obvious problems in mismanaging our emotional investments: expecting others to make us happy, repressing feelings and not resolving guilt. There are, however, sound investments to be made. What are the characteristics of good emotional investments? What can we do? Sound emotional investments follow sound thinking. When my thoughts are not focused, my emotions jump back and forth. I am more vulnerable to poor investments. Sometimes I have watched my children play Monopoly. As the struggle for survival goes on, the children begin to work on one another's minds. They try to convince each other of the value of certain property trades or purchases. Sooner or later one person will weaken or a powerful argument will be put forth and the trade will result in victory. When the game is over the loser often says something like, "I would have won, but you got me all confused." In Monopoly and in life, poor investments come out of thinking which is not based on truth. In the financial realm we turn to our stockbroker for sound advice. But in the spiritual and psychological realm straight thinking begins with the Bible.

Whether you are reading in the Old Testament or the New, there is a pattern in Scripture which provides a sound basis for emotional investments. This pattern is presented clearly in Colossians 3. The chapter begins by reminding us of what Christ has done for us. This is fundamental to any solid emotional investment program. We have been raised with Christ to new life. We have access to a whole new realm of investment. We are not limited to bonds of five and one-quarter per cent.

Next we are told to set our minds on things above (Col 3:1-2). Don't ponder poverty when you can contemplate the richness of God. When I have my focus on him, other things are not so likely to be blown out of proportion. As a friend said, "When I realized what God has done for me, the rise and fall of the stock market didn't seem important anymore." This was his way of saying his emotional investments had changed.

Colossians 3 then tells us that we are not to allow ourselves to be controlled by the things which formerly controlled us. Paul uses strong language. "Put to death, therefore, whatever belongs to your earthly nature" (Col 3:5). Don't keep investing in a lifestyle which can only lead to emotional bankruptcy. There is a better way. We are instead to put on or invest in compassion, kindness, humility, gentleness, patience and forgiveness. These don't come automatically. But if we put in the effort, we will enjoy the emotional dividends.

Paul then emphasizes letting God work. "Let the peace of Christ rule in your hearts. . . . Let the word of Christ dwell in you richly" (Col 3:15-16). There is a patience factor here. A bond does not reach maturity in one day and a new stock does not double in value overnight. We need to give them time. If we cash them in prematurely, we can lose all the gains we have made.

I love the story of Jesus calming the storm. The disciples feared for their lives. When Jesus was awakened, he calmed the storm and asked a simple but piercing question: "Where is your faith?" (Lk 8:25). Once again we return to that crucial theme. One of the most difficult things in making sound emotional investments is letting God be God, believing that he has the power to help us.

A last step in following the biblical pattern for emotional investments can be summed up in two words: "Be thankful" (Col 3:15). Ronald Allen drives home this point: "So it is with the praise of God. The one thing left for us to do is to do it. Praise is a matter of life and breath. . . . A life lived without the praise of God is not really a life worth living. It is only by a life of praise that we may respond properly to our always faithful God."[7]

The following key words and phrases summarize what Colossians 3 prescribes for making sound emotional investments:

Remember what God has done.

Focus on the things of God.

Eliminate ungodliness.

Acquire new attitudes and behaviors.

Allow God to work in you.

Praise God for all he is doing.

Investments That Paid Off

The Bible provides us not only with a pattern which leads to sound emotional investments but also with numerous examples. Let's look at three.

First is Peter in an episode we touched on in chapter five. After Peter had denied Jesus three times, Jesus appeared to him to restore him spiritually and psychologically (see Jn 21). Jesus first pushed Peter to reaffirm his love three times and told Peter he still had work to do. Jesus then made the simple command, "Follow me!" Peter invested poorly at this point. Instead of rejoicing in his renewed relationship, he began to ask about John. Jesus' response found in John 21:23 is simple: "If I want him to remain alive until I return, what is that to you?" Peter recovered from his error of comparing himself with John and refocused his emotional, intellectual and physical energies on Christ. Because of this Peter was able to preach one of the most powerful sermons in the history of the church. Acts 2 is a thrilling example of what God can do when we make good emotional investments.

A second example is Paul. In Philippians 4:12 he says, "I have learned the secret of being content in any and every situation." We are not to be controlled by circumstances. We are to be controlled by God. Investing in circumstances is a poor choice for circumstances are like mattresses. If you live under them, you will be smothered.

The final example is Jesus himself. Two important issues stand out in the description of Jesus found in Philippians 2:5-11. He had a humble but strong spirit, and he was not directed by misplaced priorities. Jesus could have demanded his rights. He could have rejected the cross. He chose, however, a better way. "Therefore God exalted Him to the highest place and gave him the name that is above every name" (Phil 2:9). The emotional payoff for Jesus was great because he didn't allow his human limitations to dictate his priorities. Philippians 2:5 says our attitude should be the same as his.

Another major help in making emotional investments is prayer. Talking or writing about prayer is easier than praying. We want emotional balance or tranquility but can't seem to get it. The reason may be found in James 4:2, "You do not have, because you do not ask God." Matthew 7:7-8 puts it in a positive perspective: "Ask and it will be given to you; seek and you will find; knock and the door will be opened to you. For everyone who asks receives; he who seeks finds; and to him who knocks, the door will be opened."

Have you ever taken the time to pray, "God, do you want me to be upset about this?" Have you ever prayed for God's help in quieting your spirit? Swihart writes, "God helps us to see ourselves more clearly and to deal with our feelings in a more honest way when we converse with him in prayer. He reveals to us our feelings and thoughts which we have dealt with dishonestly and destructively. We also need to specifically ask him to heal our emotional lives in these areas."[8]

The very act of praying is itself an emotional investment. Staying upset for long about unimportant things is hard when I come to a God who is sovereign over all. As I savor his power and love, I become stronger in the positive emotions of love, joy and peace which I need to affect those around me. Prayer is like saving money. The only way to do it is to do it. The returns are guaranteed by an agency much greater than any government.

Taking the Offensive

A third important guideline to sound emotional investment is to live a proactive (purposeful) rather than a reactive (defensive) life. A good investment firm does not wait for things to happen; it aims to make them happen. Developing plans, evaluating options, keeping options open, setting goals, striving to reach those goals: these can be frightening to some Christians because they are afraid of moving ahead of God. I share this caution, but I also have a strong belief that a moving ship is easier to guide than one tied to the dock.

Good athletes create favorable situations for themselves or their team. Recently I watched a football game in which the commentator said that the momentum seemed to be switching because the defense had been on the field too long. Defenses are almost always in a reactive mode. The offense creates the situation. We need to take the offensive by asking, "How would I like to feel about this problem? How would I like to be relating to this person?"

Mary, a client of mine, broke off several relationships which had been meaningful to her because of her fears. Through the course of counseling Mary began to trust God with her fears and one day surprised me by saying, "I'm going to have lunch with my old friend. I don't know what I will say to her except that I'm sorry for what I did. I know God will help me." When I saw Mary the next time she was thrilled. Her friend had readily accepted her apology, and they were back on track with their friendship. By taking the initiative Mary stopped the emotional drain and came to realize that she and her friend wanted the same thing. Augsburger points out:

> If we are stuck, stopped in our tracks and waiting for circumstances to change before we begin appreciating life, anticipating joy with our pain, and experiencing the richness of what is, then we are stopping ourselves. We are keeping ourselves stuck. We are riding the brakes.
>
> We can quit, when we choose. We can look for new beginnings. We can start over. Not from some past beginning, but now. We may not be able to take it from the top, but we can take it from here and now and get on with living.[9]

How's Your Portfolio?

A final factor in managing emotional investments has been referred to earlier but must be underscored. Be open to God's emotional blessing. God is as much concerned about our feelings as he is about our choices, thoughts or behaviors. Philippians 4:7 says, "The peace of God, which transcends all understanding, will guard your hearts and your minds in Christ Jesus." God will do his work. We need only to let it happen within us. We often invest poorly because we fear God will reject us if we open up to him. But Swihart writes these words of encouragement, "The bottom line for Christians is total acceptance, God's total love for us. We can risk facing any feeling in us, either in one particular situation or as part of a longer growth process. We can be secure from self-rejection knowing that God will never reject us."[10]

Take account of where you are with God. If you are one of his, relax. If you are not, then turn to God and relax.

Management of our emotional investments is possible once we decide to take control of that area of our lives. Then Scripture, prayer, setting priorities and allowing God to do his work can lead us to a quality of emotional life never before experienced. How is your portfolio?

8
Anger without Sin: Keys to Emotional Control

AS WE READ THE BIBLE WE occasionally come on statements that baffle us and seem to defy practical application. Ephesians 4:26-27 is such a statement: "In your anger do not sin: Do not let the sun go down while you are still angry, and do not give the devil a foothold." We have been trained to believe that any feelings of anger are automatically sinful. This verse suggests, however, that what we do in our anger or with our anger is the key.

When people get angry, they often say, "I just couldn't help myself. I don't know what came over me." The implication is that the anger springs from some external source, and we are only the innocent victims. If so, then God could hardly hold us responsible. True, things do happen that trigger a physiological response which we label *anger*. At the point that this signal goes from the body to the brain, we become responsible for our actions. Our response to the signal, not the signal itself, constitutes the sin. Thus, "in your anger do not sin." We choose to be angry or at least choose a response to our impulse of anger. Let's consider three causes of anger.

Hurt, Frustration and Fear

When someone hurts us physically or hurts our feelings, we often become angry. We may flare up immediately or we may think about what happened for a while and then feel angry.

The same thing happens when we are frustrated, when someone or something prevents us from reaching a goal. The anger tends to cover up the disappointment or failure we feel. It may be good in the short run because it keeps us going. In the long run, however, it will deplete our emotional energy.

Paul Hauck has outlined six levels people move through in getting angry:

1. "I want something."
2. "I didn't get what I wanted and am frustrated."
3. "It is awful and terrible not to get what I want."
4. "You shouldn't frustrate me! I must have my way."
5. "You're bad for frustrating me."
6. "Bad people ought to be punished."[1]

Use the steps to evaluate a recent episode in which you became angry. It may not fit you exactly, but you will probably find that steps 1 and 2 are true. Your perception of truth begins to break down in step 3. You don't *like* to be frustrated, but being frustrated is not as terrible as you think. The retreat to irrationality and uncontrolled anger continues with the lies you tell yourself in steps 4 through 6. Why must you have your way? Jesus didn't. Who says people are bad just because they frustrate you? Who says bad people ought to be punished? God said, "It is mine to avenge; I will repay" (Deut 32:35).

Fear also leads to anger for some people. It is a defense against the lack of control we feel when we are afraid. My father used to become angry when Mom or one of us children got hurt or was in danger. He didn't know how to deal with his fear, so he became angry. People who fear close relationships with others often become angry and drive people away. It is effective but not satisfying.

Paul Welter has developed a chart (figure 6) which shows how anger interacts with other emotions. When we are hurt, for example, our awareness of feelings grows until it levels off. Somewhere in the process we feel a second emotion which is often anger. Anger also rises in our awareness until it levels off, usually

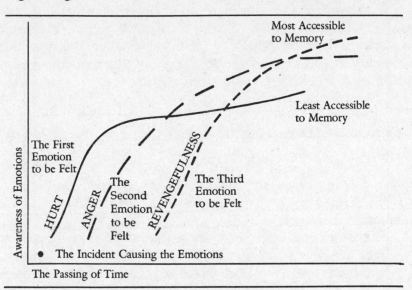

Figure 6 The Responses of Hurt, Anger and Revengefulness[2]

at a higher level than the hurt. We may be very aware of being angry with someone even though we do not know in detail how he or she hurt us. As the anger stabilizes, a third emotion can arise —revenge. It follows the same pattern and usually levels off at a higher level of awareness than the hurt or anger. We can become obsessed with thoughts of how to get back at someone.

Welter's diagram suggests a wrong decision and thus is an example of turning anger into the sin of revenge. Revenge never resolves hurt and neither does anger. Revenge is fighting fire with fire. Undoubtedly this is one reason why Jesus said to turn the other cheek.

The key to emotional control is to be aware of the different feelings as they arise and to deal with them individually instead of letting one emotion pile on another. When we realize that we are angry, the decision is ours as to how to control our reactions. Talking rationally with the person who hurt you can resolve the issue in a way that anger and revenge cannot.

Welter's diagram can help us understand Ephesians 4:26-27. It suggests that when we become aware of our anger, we should not sin by harboring it. (Don't let the sun go down on your wrath.) Neither should we sin by choosing revenge to resolve the hurt. This would indeed "give the devil a foothold."

In the Sermon on the Mount Jesus instructed us to go to the brother who has something against us and be reconciled quickly. Interestingly, he does not say to go to the person we have something against. The solution for that is to forgive him or her, a topic I will deal with later in this chapter. If, however, we don't help people who are angry with us to resolve the issue, we may allow them to remain in their anger and commit murder in their minds.

The issue is to resolve hostility whenever possible. Forgiving others and facing serious charges against us are both difficult. But our gifts to God are readily received only when we have done everything we can to restore relationships with our brothers and sisters. Whether we feel others should have been offended doesn't matter. Analyzing the situation to death is a waste of time. We simply need to start over with a clean slate.

I must caution, however, that we cannot demand a forgiving response from those we have offended. We can only humbly and prayerfully ask to be forgiven. Give them and the Holy Spirit time and space to bring about healing. Stay accessible but do not put demands on them for immediate reconciliation.

When anger is due to frustration, telling the other person about your feelings is usually helpful. Sometimes we need to let such people know that they are the victims of our anger and not the villains. If I am thwarted in my efforts toward some goal I may take it out on my wife or apartment mate. When I catch myself, I need to acknowledge this sin and draw closer to the offended person. Sometimes it is helpful to say, "I wish I had responded more warmly to you even if I was frustrated." Often the person you offended will respond warmly to such openness by asking, "What can I do to help?"

Another way to deal with anger stemming from frustration is to change our focus from the problem to a new course of action. If we dwell on past failures we only relive our agony and rekindle anger. On the other hand when we focus on future possibilities, we rekindle hope.

When anger results from fear it is usually a smokescreen hiding the real issue—our specific fear. When people I counsel tell me about a destructive episode of anger, they are often amazed that I respond by asking them to tell me about their fear during the episode. "How did you know I was afraid?" they ask. If one is afraid of intimacy, what better way to keep people at a distance than to become angry? If you are afraid of defeat, you can hide behind anger. That will certainly give you an explanation for your failure. If you are afraid of being hurt, your anger can hurt other people before they hurt you. The list could go on.

Becoming angry when fearful only leads to greater frustration since the fear has not been addressed properly. However, when I acknowledge fear, I can allow the resources of God and of other people to meet me at my point of need. My fear won't be cured by accident. When I am energized by anger, I need to choose constructive means of dealing with the fear that caused the anger.

Although only three causes of anger have been discussed here (hurt, frustration and fear), there are obviously others. Our search for better control begins when we ask God to help us discover the specific causes of our anger.

Is there anything we can do if we feel bombarded by impulses of anger? Can anger be controlled or is it always the controller? The model which follows may help to answer these questions.

Keys to Control

Awareness is the first key to bringing any emotion under control. In the case of anger, awareness begins by knowing one's body. Headaches, tremors, upset stomach, tiredness, nervousness are often signs of anger. Such signals may come from any part of the body at any time. The more you become aware of the physical signals your body is giving, the greater the chance of taking steps toward controlling your anger.

DeLoss Friesen has suggested looking at emotional control from the perspective of figure 7. This illustrates the period of time between becoming aware of our anger and our losing control, the moment when we can do something productive with our angry impulses. As the level of arousal gets higher, it crosses an imaginary line after which we are no longer in control. At that point we may be shouting things we may not even believe or striking out physically at someone. To increase our control and enlarge the opportunity for effective action we must increase the space between the dotted lines, either lowering our awareness threshold (learning to become aware of our angry feelings earlier) or raising the level at which we lose control.

This can be done by positive self-talk such as, "I'm feeling really angry, but I do not have to give in to these feelings. I may be hot, but I don't have to blow. I want to choose my reaction rather than let my blood pressure dictate my response. I can also ask myself whether the situation is worth the energy I am expending on the experience.

As I have become aware of my own anger, I have also found it helpful to ask questions of the person my anger is directed at instead of making irrational statements I will regret later. "Did you

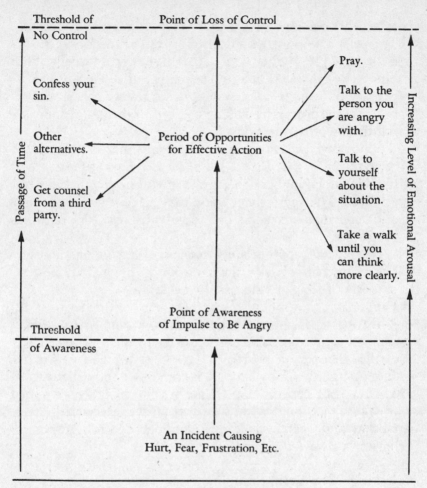

Figure 7 Possible Results of an Impulse to Be Angry

do (say) that because you are angry with me or because you are trying to hurt me or because you didn't know how I would feel about it?"

In their classic book on assertiveness, Alberti and Emmons draw a careful distinction between being assertive (saying what you want or what you dislike) and becoming aggressive (punishing the other person for his or her failure to meet your needs).

The person who carries a desire for self-expression to the extreme of aggressive behavior accomplishes goals usually at the expense of others. Although frequently self-enhancing and expressive of feelings in the situation, aggressive behavior hurts others in the process by making choices for them, and minimizing their worth as persons.

Aggressive behavior commonly results in a "put down" of the receiver. Rights denied, she or he feels hurt, defensive, and humiliated. His or her goals in the situation, of course, are not achieved. The aggressive person may achieve goals, but may also generate hatred and frustration which may later return as vengeance.

In contrast, appropriately assertive behavior in the same situation would be self-enhancing for the actor, an honest expression of feelings, and usually achieve goals.[3]

If I am unable to distinguish whether or not my behavior is aggressive or assertive, a simple question or two might help. Did my statements seem reasonable to me and to the other people? Did I leave the other person intact or did my behavior tend to strip her or him of dignity? Colossians 4:6 is an excellent guideline to follow. "Let your conversation be always full of grace, seasoned with salt, so that you may know how to answer everyone." Assertive behavior or speech can lead to emotional control. Aggressive behavior is always counterproductive.

Checking Your Trail, Stopping Your Thoughts

Another key to gaining emotional control is to practice checking your trail, looking where you have been. Review how you might have responded differently. I have a history of losing my temper each time I try to purchase a new automobile. On one occasion my wife walked home because she was embarrassed to be seen with me. Trail checking was helpful. When I relived the experience I was able to identify where I lost control—when people put pressure on me. Either I need to avoid the pressure of the salesperson or tell myself something to help get over that. For instance, I do better when I stop long enough to say, "Here it comes. I hate this but I don't have to take it personally. If he really thinks I'm stupid, he wouldn't need to use all this pressure." Trail checking helped me enough that Sandy rode home with me after our last car purchase.

Positive trail checking is just as important as negative trail checking. Remind yourself of the things that you do right which lead to control. I walked into the kitchen one day just after one of my sons had been in an argument with his mother. "I better get out of here," he said to himself. "I do better when I don't try to talk when I'm mad." We can all benefit from acknowledging, practicing and perfecting changes which lead to self-control.

Successful emotional control also depends on thought stopping. Thought stopping means exactly that. Stop the thought! Stop right in the middle of the thought or, better yet, stop before beginning to move toward the thought. Any interruption such as a loud noise or an unexpected sight may change your thinking. Even so, simply deciding to not think something is not always so simple. You may have to create your own interruption or distraction if you want to practice thought stopping. I often use a rubber band that I wear loosely around my wrist. When an undesired thought comes, I give myself a flip with the band. Even though I know where the pain comes from, it serves to divert my attention long enough to get me back on a more productive track. This will only work, however, if you are committed to keeping your thinking in control.

A client who was troubled with lustful thoughts was taught to use this technique. After two weeks he had had little or no success. His counselor asked him to role play a typical situation. When it came time to stop the thought, the client almost whispered the words, "Stop it now." The counselor asked him to repeat the same scene, only this time the counselor yelled in his ear, "STOP!! I've got better things to think about." The client got the message, and he was on his way to regaining some of the emotional control he desired.

A whisper might be in order if you are trying to control anger. The key in either instance is to be persistent in not following the undesired thought through to completion. Each completion only strengthens the thought and the emotions supported by the thought.

Closely related to thought stopping is substituting actions. When I am angry I need to look for something else I can do. These substitutes should preclude the expression of the anger. For example, instead of telling the car salesperson how angry I am, I might tell him that he did a good job of showing me the car even though we were not able to reach an agreement.

To be effective, substitutes we choose for expressing our feelings need to be carefully selected. Gordon McMinn states: "A major premise has been that feelings are to be acted on, not bottled up. One word of caution must be given. Not all feelings should be indulged. Feelings become self-destructive when they fail to meet two conditions: First, feelings should be based on sound thinking, and second, feelings should result in responsible action. Unless these conditions are met, feelings do not contribute to balanced growth."[4] When you know the expression of feelings will not lead to balanced growth there is a need to look for a substitute expression. This is a critical opportunity to be who God wants you to be.

Another way to keep our emotional expressions in line is stimulus control. A stimulus is an object or event that has or may have an effect on our behavior. For example, the sight of a green traffic light is a stimulus to press on the accelerator of the car. Hearing a friend's voice may stimulate us to look for him or her at a party. Stimulus control is regulating our stimuli so we do not put ourselves in a position of having to react to all people and events.

Suppose you had been in a competition at a state fair and lost. After that the very sights or sounds of the fairgrounds might serve as stimuli to arouse your hurt and anger. If you want to control your anger, avoid these stimuli until you have had a chance to develop a better alternative response.

Talking to certain people may stimulate your anger. If you find yourself angry after spending time with certain people try to identify the point at which the anger begins. Once you identify those triggers, you are in a much better position to control the stimuli. Look ahead and you will avoid many unhappy situations.

Too often we assume that the best way to get over being angry is to talk about it. Freudian psychology tells us that the psychic energy of anger must be released. This is only half true. Dealing with anger is better than keeping anger bottled up. However, sometimes talking to scores of people about it and never talking directly to the person we have the problem with can stimulate feelings of anger even more. Also, we are in danger of pulling others into our mire of anger or gossip.

The Payoff for Anger

If we are to control our anger, or any other emotion for that matter, we need to understand the payoff which being angry has. People harbor and feed anger because they like the rewards they get from being angry. How can anything so upsetting feel good? The following examples may help.

Jim is noted for his short fuse. In fact, people around him are usually uneasy because they never know what may make him blow. But look at what happens after he gets upset. Everyone seems to come to his aid. Every effort is made to make his life more comfortable. He receives soothing words and affirmation from his fiancée, his friends, his family and his coworkers. Jim's payoff is power and attention.

Mildred is often angry with men. She readily acknowledges this. Her actions indicate she wants to be close to men, but every time they try to approach, she seems to burn them. Mildred is afraid of being rejected. The payoff for her anger is that no one can reject her, because she rejects them first. Her anger keeps her from having to face her fears, but it also keeps her from what she wants very much—male friends.

Don gets angry when he doesn't know what else to do. When he has thought through situations or dealt with circumstances before, he rarely shows anger. When he is thrown into a new situation, however, look out. He will lower his anxiety by blowing up. After all, blowing up is something he does know how to do well.

My father, like Don, used to bawl out people when they would hurt themselves. This reduced his anxiety at the sight of blood and was a substitute for giving comfort, which he only became skilled at later in life.

Analyze your anger to see what the payoff is for you. Look for a more acceptable, and less destructive, way to get the same payoff. This may be painful, but it is essential if you are to control the anger. Enlist the help of a kind but honest friend who will help guide you to a new approach.

Forgiveness: Returning Good
Any treatment of emotional control of anger would be incomplete from a Christian perspective without emphasizing the importance of forgiveness. To forgive the other person not only releases him or her but also releases you from the tyranny of your own anger. Colgrove, Bloomfield and McWilliams have a short but profound treatment of forgiveness.

> Whenever you can, as soon as you can, forgive the other person. To forgive means not just "to pardon." Originally it meant to return good treatment for ill usage.
>
> You have been ill-used. As soon as you can return good to the ill-user, without contrivance or compulsion, you are finally free.[5]

Surprisingly, the key to forgiving and being free is not to forget the offense. You may have been ill-used. You need to acknowledge that. True forgiveness is manifest when you return good to those who did you wrong. Consider the ultimate example of One who returned good to the ill-user. When you find forgiving hard, contemplate this: "But God demonstrates his own love for us in this: While we were still sinners, Christ died for us" (Rom 5:8).

To forgive means I no longer choose to look at you through the glasses of your offense. I deliberately take those off to see you differently. We hold up an ideal which may be impossible. You may never be able to forget. You can, however, forgive and set aside thoughts of the person's offense. You must also set aside thoughts of "poor me." Self-pity only leads to renewed anger and a choice to again put on the glasses of the person's offense. Such thoughts can become an obsession which will destroy you.

When my wife is hurt by someone, I sometimes use that as a stimulus to be angry at the same person. Recently, when she was struggling to forgive the person who had hurt her, I went into a tirade. I was going to set that person straight. Sandy stopped me cold by saying, "Your anger makes it more difficult for me to set aside mine." I became convicted of my own unforgiving spirit and was then able to listen as she talked through some ways she could handle the situation. This was a great lesson. We must be supportive of each other in our attempts to forgive and unhook from anger. Rescuing our friends from the offender or venting our own anger is not one such way.

In his excellent book, *Caring Enough to Forgive,* David Augsburger has outlined aspects of the forgiving process which are necessary if anger is to be replaced by more productive behavior.

Forgiveness is letting what was, be gone; what will be, come and what is now, be.

In forgiving, I finish my demands on past predicaments, problems, failures and say good-by to them with finality. I cancel my predictions, suspicions, premonitions of future failure and welcome the next moment with openness to discover what will be. I make a new transaction of affirming integrity between us now.

Finishing my demands on your past acts and words requires sorting them out and making appropriate decisions. Those demands which are just can be negotiated until we reach the solution most satisfactory to both of us. Those demands which are pretentious, impossible and unjust can be cancelled.[6]

What have we said then about controlling our emotions? First and most important, control is possible! Not only is it possible, it is a must! We begin by acknowledging our emotions, progress to analyzing them and their effects and then exercise control in those areas where it is needed. Look for the hurt, the frustration, the fear behind the anger. Look for the payoffs. Look for the cues that trigger your emotions. When you find them, avoid them until you have grown beyond them.

Lastly, remember that anger is not just a psychological problem; it is a spiritual problem. It requires the resources of God. God has commanded us not to sin in our anger. He loves to provide us with the means to accomplish the task. In the same context as the instruction regarding control of anger, these words of encouragement are given: "Be kind and compassionate to one another, forgiving each other, just as in Christ God forgave you. Be imitators of God, therefore, as dearly loved children and live a life of love, just as Christ loved us and gave himself up for us as a fragrant offering and sacrifice to God" (Eph 4:32—5:2).

9
The
Release of
Forgiveness

IN PREVIOUS CHAPTERS I MADE casual reference to the role of forgiveness in healthy personality growth. In this chapter I will expand on those ideas and specify some of the issues which make forgiving so difficult.

Forgiveness can be viewed as a three-component process—past, present and future.

Past: Release the other person. Release yourself from the past offense.

Present: Commit yourself to being open to that person right now.

Future: Resist the temptation to view future interactions from the perspective of the past.

The Past Tense of Forgiveness

Forgiveness only comes with a full awareness of the sin. I have been hurt; I have been slighted. I cannot truly forgive until I have assessed the damage. Releasing the other person does not deny the damage. True release requires that I tell it like it is. "You hurt me, but I am no longer choosing to view you or our relationship through the filter of that hurt."

Releasing also means we stop trying to make other people pay for their sins. Our revengeful spirits tell us that we would feel better if those who hurt us suffered just a little bit. This is not true. In fact, the opposite is true. The more we try to make others pay, the deeper we get caught in negative feelings and reliving the offense. The cost of sin is so great that only the death of the God-man himself—Jesus—could pay the price. Resist the temptation to extract a pound of flesh from offenders even when they appear flippant about being forgiven. Their flippancy may just be nervousness about being released.

Why is releasing so difficult? Often we cannot release others because we haven't released ourselves. Invariably when we have been hurt by someone else, we will be bombarded by if-only-I-hadn't thinking. "If I had just warned him, he might not have wrecked my car." "If only I hadn't started the argument, she might not have left." Thinking that we are responsible for the past keeps us glued to the past and prevents us from releasing others from the past.

In addition to releasing ourselves from the responsibility of the past, we also need to release ourselves from the regrets of the past. Grieving over the losses we have suffered because of an offense is easy. But each time we recount our losses we run the risk of re-kindling our unforgiving spirit. This will only result in crippling our spirits which will eventually cause even deeper loss. Forgiveness requires that we assess the loss, assign the blame, release the blame and start looking to the future.

Finally, releasing ourselves from the past means letting go of the hurt and anger we feel because of the offense. When we are still immersed in anger, we slip back into reliving the event. Anger also results in trying to make others pay for their sins. The return of compassion for them is usually a sign that we have forgiven. Love "is not easily angered, it keeps no record of wrongs" (1 Cor 13:5). If you are struggling with anger and an inability to forgive, you may wish to reread chapter eight to grasp some of the keys to controlling this emotion.

The Present Tense of Forgiveness

Leaving the past without a sense of where we are going is difficult. The present tense of forgiveness requires that we be open to the injured relationship right now. Notice, I did not say that we immediately commit ourselves to the relationship. We commit ourselves to be open to that person. The relationship may or may not develop. The key is to be available to God and allow him to do what he wants in our lives. Sometimes there are personality differences which make relationship building difficult. Indeed, these differences may have contributed to the offense in the first place. If we remain open to God, he may choose to change us or the other party. If we expect great things from God, we may be wonderfully delighted by the way our enemy can become our friend.

When I first entered Bible college I found that I was easily offended. Some of the offenses could be attributed to my oversensitivity, and other offenses could be attributed to the lack of sensitivity on the part of other students. I remember being constantly upset by Norman. Several times he hurt me, and what made it worse was he didn't even seem to be aware that he did it. I tried to forgive and I tried to remain open to him.

As my hurt and anger subsided, a relationship began to develop. He wasn't such a bad person after all. Also I became aware that not all of the problem was his. I was supersensitive and jealous. He knew more about baseball than I did, and he wouldn't let me play the expert all the time. Once I admitted this pettiness we had some great conversations. He became a loyal friend who even stayed up half the night to type one of my term papers. If I had not remained open to the possibility of a relationship, I would have lost a lot. Good friends aren't that easy to find.

The Future Tense of Forgiveness

The future tense of forgiveness is trust. Once I have stopped blaming someone for a past hurt and have opened myself to him or her in the present, I am free to trust for the future. If you have been hurt repeatedly by another person, you may feel vulnerable as you read this. No one likes to be hurt again. We must balance these fears with the broad scriptural principle that if we try to keep our lives we will lose them, and if we lose our lives for Christ's sake, we will gain them. Living a meaningful life is a risky business.

I am impressed with the risks that Jesus was willing to take with his friend Peter. Peter had denied Jesus three times and had stayed away from Jesus' crucifixion. After the resurrection Jesus appeared to Peter and six other disciples while they were fishing at Tiberias. After helping them catch and cook fish for breakfast, Jesus began the work of re-establishing an open relationship with Peter. One thing stands out clearly: Jesus wanted Peter to know that he trusted him despite the denials. So he entrusted to Peter an important work to do. "Feed my sheep. . . . Follow me" (Jn 21:17, 19). Such active trust is difficult when we have been hurt by another person, but Jesus shows us the way.

Being trusted by Jesus gave Peter the courage to go forward. He was complete again. History records that he proved worthy of that trust. People usually do live up to the level of trust that others have in them. The burden is on the one who forgives to allow the forgiveness to be complete and the life-giving trust to be re-established.

In twenty years of counseling with college students I have encountered hundreds who feel worthless because they have been told by parents or friends that they have been forgiven, but the trust has not been re-established. This leaves them feeling hollow, scarcely alive. In trusting others we risk being hurt, but we also receive the joy of watching some come back to life as they realize the trust we have in them.

As a child I did a number of things of which I am not very proud. While my father disciplined me for these acts, he never withheld trust. I lived with the consequences of my behavior, but I was never put on the shelf. He believed that I wanted to do better and gave me the opportunity to prove that I did. I am eternally grateful for such love.

Forgiveness is an act of love. It is giving someone the gift of life. It is fresh air, flowers, excitement and quiet tears. It is also reciprocal because when we give the gift of forgiveness, we also receive. As we free others, we become more free ourselves. I once stopped a child who was skipping down the street to ask him why he was so happy. "My daddy's not mad at me anymore," he said and kept right on skipping. As a father, I know there was a skip in his daddy's step too.

"How do I learn to forgive?" The answer is simple. Begin to do it. As we do God will help us to release others and ourselves from the past, to be open in the present and to trust in the future. Forgiveness is a matter of faith. We will not forgive perfectly; only God can do that. But we can forgive as much as we can, as soon as we can, as often as we need to. In the process we will find more pleasure in loving than in punishing the offender.

Forgiveness is an act of the will and requires great persistence. Jesus was not making idle chatter when he talked of the need to forgive seventy times seven. Satan will continuously bring past offenses to our minds to undermine our relationships. We need to resist him by forgiving each time the offense comes to mind. We can imagine the face of the person to whom we are extending forgiveness changing from a frown to a smile as we clasp hands. I believe that some of the happiest moments in the life of Jesus occurred when he released his offenders. Even in the great agony he suffered just before he died, he forgave the criminal next to him on the cross and prayed for his tormentors, "Father, forgive them, for they do not know what they are doing" (Lk 23:34).

Recently, Sandy and I sat discussing forgiveness (probably following a "forgiving session" with one another). We were quick to realize that forgiving is not to be contingent on being asked for forgiveness. I am to forgive whether she asks me to forgive or not. This is hard because if she doesn't ask for forgiveness, how do I know she is repentant? How do I know that she has paid for her sins internally? When I ask myself this, I have already missed the point. It does not matter whether the person who has offended me has paid the price. The point is that I am to forgive as God forgives. "Be kind and compassionate to one another, forgiving each other, just as in Christ God forgave you" (Eph 4:32).

God forgives out of his perfection because Christ paid. We need to forgive out of our imperfection realizing too that Jesus paid for their sins. In other words, as believers we need to apply the principle of grace to those who offend us. That is such a better way to live. I don't have to wait until Sandy confesses her offense to me to release her and to release myself. I can do this as soon as I feel hurt. Then I am free to relate openly with her moment by moment. This has done wonders to preserve the good times between us. The release may not be permanent because I may not have assessed all the damage, but I can forgive again as I feel the offense more deeply. Great healing results both for me and the person who offended me.

The Other Side of Forgiveness

Thus far we have focused on the importance of forgiving the other person. But sometimes we are on the other side of forgiveness, the side of being the offender. When we have offended someone, we need to acknowledge that offense and to confess it to God and to the party we have offended. This frees us to relate openly to that person and allows us to release ourselves emotionally from the offense.

Like children, we find it difficult to admit that we are wrong. When we do, we often rationalize away the need to go to the other person. This is in direct violation of the teachings of Jesus in the

Sermon on the Mount: "Therefore, if you are offering your gift at the altar and there remember that your brother has something against you, leave your gift there in front of the altar. First go and be reconciled to your brother; then come and offer your gift" (Mt 5:23-24). Taking the initiative in re-establishing the relationship serves two functions. We release the brother from the temptation to seek revenge (murder or slander, see Mt 5:21-22) and we free ourselves to give God our full attention as we offer our gifts before the altar. We need to be concerned for the tolerance level of others and help them release their anger toward us. Saying "I didn't mean to make Mary angry" isn't enough. Neither is "If Tom's offended, that's just his problem." Jesus wants more from us than that because he wants us to dwell together in unity (see Ps 133:1). Failure to do so weakens the relationship and robs us of our spiritual vitality. I speak from experience.

A number of years ago, when my mother died, I offended a friend by asking him, through a third party, if I could borrow some money. Jim loaned me the money but was deeply hurt that I had not called him directly. Even though I could rationalize my behavior and tell you all the reasons for what I did, I was wrong and my friend was hurt.

I complicated the situation further by taking some non-Christian advice from another Christian friend who said, "Don't worry about it. He'll get over it." He didn't get over it, and even though God repeatedly prompted me to go to him, I refused.

The more time passed, the more afraid and reluctant I became. Jim and I still saw each other occasionally, but it just wasn't the kind of relationship we had before. I continued to withdraw and remained disobedient despite the fact that I too was hurting inside. This pattern continued for almost three years. I tried to keep walking with the Lord, but my Christian life was numb and listless. Each opportunity I had to speak to Jim—and did not—increased the inner deadness. I began to wonder how long God would put up with my stubborn, fearful behavior.

The answer came in a strange way. God forced me into a situation where I again had to ask Jim for some money, this time for a missions project. This threw us back into contact with one another, and in the process I apologized. The relationship was restored. I remember his words as he extended his hand to me, "Thanks for having enough guts to ask." Little did he know it was as though I had no choice. God forced me to risk losing the relationship forever instead of allowing it to remain unhealthy because of my failure to apologize. In the end I got my friend back. Afterward I realized how foolish I had been and how much I had needed Jim's forgiveness. Our heavenly Father truly knows how to care for those who cannot or will not care for themselves. There is no greater miracle than forgiving and being forgiven. Thank you, Jim! Thank you, God!

Lest you lose the lesson in the story, here is what I learned:

1. God clearly wants us to be responsible for seeking forgiveness from those we have offended.

2. This is difficult to do because our pride often gets in the way.

3. Procrastination leads to further sins of disobedience. Confession is never going to be easier than it is right now.

4. God is lovingly persistent in his demands that we obey him.

5. God delights in restoring broken and battered relationships.

6. We don't need to be afraid to trust God. He is trustworthy! He often does for us what we refuse to do for ourselves.

As I have thought about the two sides of forgiveness—forgiving and receiving forgiveness—I have realized that faith is required to do both. Without faith in God's care and protection, I cannot forgive another person. Without faith I cannot go to another person or to God to receive forgiveness. The fear of being punished is too great. With faith, however, both are readily available to me.

I have wondered, Is it better to give or to receive? My conclusion is this: It is better to give *and* to receive. This is God's plan for our wholeness.

10
Self-Esteem: God Don't Make No Junk

EARLIER I SAID THAT EMOTIONS are an important part of being "fearfully and wonderfully made." Is that just theory? What can we say to the parade of hurting people we meet? How are they managing their feelings?

Janna is twenty-seven and reports that she does not remember a day in her life in which she was not gripped by the fear of abandonment. John, age thirty-three, reports that although he received Christ as Savior during childhood, he has never experienced the fact that God loves him. David, eighteen, is torn by the shattering awareness that his father is having an affair with another woman. June, who is sixteen, is a victim of the advances of an incestuous father. Marsha, in her early twenties, recently divorced, is all alone. Tim, fifteen, is bombarded by guilt as he struggles with sexual temptation.

We can easily identify them as people in deep psychological and spiritual pain. We are moved by their agony. The pain others feel may be more subtle and yet just as real. They weep because of failure, withdraw because of disappointment, shout angrily because of hurt. Some suffer silently because they are afraid that the cry for help will fall on deaf ears. Many question their relationship with God, or even the existence or value of a God who seems far away. Others drift from group to group hoping to find solace in human comfort.

Such hurts greatly affect the way we view ourselves. Many believe their pain is retribution for sin. God zaps those who step out of line, you know. But Jesus' view, as revealed in his encounter with a blind man, is much different. "As he went along, he saw a man blind from birth. His disciples asked him, 'Rabbi, who sinned, this man or his parents, that he was born blind?' 'Neither this man nor his parents sinned,' said Jesus, 'but this happened so that the work of God might be displayed in his life' " (Jn 9:1-3). After saying this Jesus healed the man of his blindness. Suffering as punishment is refuted while he emphasizes the importance of God working in us in the midst of our suffering.

My colleague, Loren Fischer of Western Conservative Baptist Seminary, puts it this way, "God loves us too much to waste pain!" Despite this truth, our self-esteem struggles with pain. Emotions interpret our worth rather than facts. We feel alone in our pain and grief. But as Swindoll writes, "A teardrop on earth summons the King of Heaven. Rather than being ashamed or disappointed, the Lord takes note of our inner friction when hard times are oiled by tears. He turns these situations into moments of tenderness; He never forgets those crises in our lives where tears were shed."[1]

Unruly emotions are certainly not the only cause of low self-esteem. In figure 8 Bruce Narramore suggests four components of a positive self-concept and compares them with the elements of a negative view of self.[2]

Positive Self-Concept	Negative Self-Concept
Sense of Significance and Worth	Feeling of Badness, Worthlessness
Attitude of Confidence	Anxiety and Feelings of Inferiority
Feelings of Security	Insecurity and Worry
Awareness of Being Loved	Loneliness, Isolation and Depression

Figure 8 Positive and Negative Self-Concepts

In the remainder of this chapter we will examine some of the hindrances to self-esteem and show how they destroy one or more of the components of a healthy self-concept. Then we will look at the ways in which faith can be expressed to allow God not only to remove the hindrances but also to strengthen the components of a positive self-concept.

Conditional Love
The hindrances to self-esteem are many. Theoretically, any event (whether private, such as being embarrassed by a thought you entertain, or public, such as being reprimanded before the entire class for being tardy) may affect our self-esteem. Unfortunately, we do not always judge ourselves by the preponderance of evidence. Our propensity for negative thinking may result in low self-esteem even in the face of evidence which suggests worth, competence, security and love. We are molded by both what we bring into life, and the experiences of life. Self-esteem is affected by both hereditary factors such as temperament and environmental factors such as the situations we find ourselves in. I will focus primarily on the hindrances to self-esteem that result from our relationships with significant others, our internal struggles and our relationship (or lack of it) with our Creator.

The first hindrance to self-esteem is that we have been trained in conditional love. Although most parents do not intend to do so, they often convey love to their children in a confusing way. The verbal message is usually straight—"I love you." The non-verbal messages are not so clear. We tend to ignore people when they do things we like and to punish them when they violate our standards. This confuses children. When they are ignored they feel that they didn't meet the standards. Why else would the parents not acknowledge the behavior? On the other hand, the punishment for not meeting the mark leads to a belief that love is available only when you do good. This is the root of conditional love. Children grow up believing that they are loved only because of what they do and not because of who they are. There is no feeling of worth when you have been trained in conditional love. There is only a sense of failure that says, "I'll never make it."

Contrast this with the potential for feelings of worth that come from being loved unconditionally. John Powell writes, "Unconditional love means that I cannot always predict my reaction or guarantee my strength, but one thing is certain: I am committed to your growth and happiness. I will always accept you. I will always love you."[3] When I feel accepted and actively loved, I feel worthy. Thus Powell writes, "The only genuine love worthy of the name is unconditional."

Conditional love also affects Narramore's other three components of self-esteem: attitudes of confidence, feelings of security and awareness of being loved. First, self-confidence, or a feeling of competence, does not develop under conditional love because the person in power keeps changing the rules of the game presumably to prompt greater levels of performance. Parents often unwittingly, but diabolically and destructively, play the moving-target game. A child strives to meet their expectations only to be met with a new challenge rather than acceptance based on what has been done. School grades are a good example. If Terry starts out with a C, he may mistakenly believe that his parents will love him more when he improves. His spirit is dashed, however, when he gets a B only to have a parent say, "I don't understand why you can't get A's. Jimmy Michaels does."

Second, when love is conditional, security is also a problem. Our friend Janna, who led the parade of hurting people at the beginning of the chapter, was constantly told to do better, but never told that she was okay.

Third, I have found great joy in seeing the heavy emphasis in Scripture on God's love for us. Romans 5:8-11 and 1 John 5:1-12 are only two of many such passages to revel in. God loves us too much to leave our relationship with him in doubt. "God demonstrates his own love for us in this: While we were still sinners, Christ died for us. Since we have now been justified by his blood, how much more shall we be saved from God's wrath through him" (Rom 5:8-9). Conditional love begets despair and loneliness and an inability to express love to others. Love begets love.

If your problems with self-esteem result from being trained under conditional love standards, you can start over. Begin by reading the passages mentioned above. There is a better way, and God is that better way. Some of God's people may also be able to show you a better way if you take the risk of getting close. As Jesus said, "A new commandment I give you: Love one another. As I have loved you, so you must love one another. All men will know that you are my disciples if you love one another" (Jn 13:34-35).

Perfectionism

Unconditional love leads directly to a second hindrance to positive self-esteem, perfectionism. Perfectionists are unable to accept any of their behavior unless they see it as being absolutely correct. I saw this in my son after he had just won a district cross-country meet with fifty-two participants. As he put his sweat clothes back on he said, "I finally found a sport that I am good at." I was startled. What about his wrestling and basketball accomplishments? He even had one championship. Didn't that account for anything? I realized that at that stage in his life winning was everything. He was plagued with perfectionism. I shuddered as I realized how his perfectionism had robbed him of the joy of previous accomplishments.

Scripture emphasizes improvement, not perfection. After making a lengthy list of qualities (faith, goodness, knowledge, self-control, perseverance, godliness, brotherly kindness and love) which we should possess, Peter wrote, "For if you possess these qualities in increasing measure, they will keep you from being ineffective and unproductive in your knowledge of our Lord Jesus Christ" (2 Pet 1:8). The emphasis is that growth thwarts the inertia of perfectionism. Even in those verses where we are commanded to be perfect (such as Mt 5:48, Jn 17:23 and Eph 4:13) the emphasis is on maturity and completeness.

I have several friends who are artists. I was surprised when I first saw their work. Instead of sharing my joy and excitement, they seemed embarrassed and uneasy. At first I discounted their behavior as shyness or nervousness about being accepted. Later I realized that the problem was deeper. They were unable to receive joy from their work and unable to share their work with others because of a crippling perfectionism which tried to discredit all my compliments.

In his book *How to Do What You Want to Do,* Paul Hauck has pinpointed the crux of perfectionism. "The major lesson to be learned is that it is more important to do than to do well. Stop playing God, stop insisting how good everything has to be that you attempt, and realize once and for all that everything has a beginning. You usually do badly in the beginning, and you are no different from anybody else. So start where you are and keep trying until you get better by slow degrees."[4]

How does perfectionism affect the four areas of positive self-concept? Perfectionism, like conditional love, destroys feelings of worth because if we only feel worthy when we have achieved perfection, we will only feel worthy one time in a thousand. The effect on feelings of confidence is just as devastating. Perfectionism robs us of the awareness of what God has equipped us to do.

When I was a high-school student, a teacher pulled me aside and said, "I hope I can help you not be like your cousin. He was the most gifted student in my class, but I couldn't get him to relax and enjoy it. He had so much talent, yet he wouldn't use it because he was afraid he wouldn't be good enough." I told him he didn't have to worry and showed him so many mistakes he was probably sorry he opened his mouth.

Feeling secure is also hard when we constantly judge ourselves by the yardstick of perfection. In fact, we don't even feel secure with ourselves, let alone with others. When we try to do perfectly and fail, as we will, we don't even trust ourselves. When this trust is gone, the security in all other relationships, including our relationship with God, is undermined.

Lastly, perfectionism undermines our awareness of being loved because of self-inflicted loneliness and isolation. One Sunday at church I approached Scott and Barbara, friends in a small group with us. Noticing Barbara's smile I said, "You look lovely today, Barbara." She blushed, began touching her dress and said, "Oh, this is just my Easter dress from last year." I said, "I don't think you heard me. I said you look lovely today." As she stood there, not knowing what to say, her husband turned to me and said, "She doesn't hear it when I say it either." Barbara's perfectionism had even caused her to be unable to receive expressions of praise.

Lack of Self-Respect
A third area which hinders positive self-concept is lack of self-respect. Self-respect relates directly to how I value what I do. It is one component of self-concept. If I do not value what I do, the value I place on my total self will be lowered. There are three prominent, interrelated causes of lack of self-respect.

The first is a failure to meet my internalized standards. I don't like or respect myself when I fail to do the kinds of things I want to do. The other side of the coin is I don't like myself when I do what I know to be wrong. Poor choices have led to disappointment in myself. No matter how skilled I may be at rationalizing, the bottom line is this: when I violate my standards for myself, I will not respect myself. I will not feel better about myself until I begin to do what I really want to do to meet my standards.

One of my first counseling clients was a college sophomore who was suffering from severe depression. As we talked she told me how depressed she was because she had not been able to do her assignments. I got up, opened the door and told her to go study. I invited her to come back when the work was finished. When she returned she felt much better. Self-respect is a great cure for depression.

A second reason we may not respect ourselves is a failure to distinguish between earned guilt (when I have done wrong) and unearned guilt (when I accept punishment for something which was not wrong or over which I did not have control). I may feel badly that I was out of town when my mother fell and broke her hip. This is unearned guilt. If on the other hand she tripped on my collection of marbles that I had left on the stairs, I may have every reason to feel guilt and lack of self-respect.

Branden has written, "One of the worst wrongs a man can do to himself is to accept an unearned guilt on the premise of a 'somehow—somehow I should know,' 'somehow I should be able to do it'—when there is no cognitive content to that 'somehow,' only an empty, undefined charge supported by nothing."[5]

We may also harbor feelings of guilt because of fear of failure. We have not done anything for which we stand condemned, yet we stand under self-condemnation. When I was growing up I often felt guilty because I didn't have confidence in boy-girl relationships. I was inexperienced but I treated myself as though I were a failure. I was falsely labeling my fears as though I had already failed. Karen Horney writes, "Thus if guilt feelings are carefully examined and are tested for genuineness, it becomes apparent that much of what looks like feelings of guilt is the expression either of anxiety or of a defense against it."[6]

If guilt is earned we will have an answer to one of the following questions: What thought or act did I do which was wrong?

Whom have I sinned against? If I were to confess my sin and ask for forgiveness, to whom would I go? If guilt is unearned, however, we may simply find that we have let ourselves down. If this is the case, choosing to do something different or trying again is the correct response. Guilt is not. Failure to live up to our own expectations is disappointing but should only produce guilt when it is sin, not when our humanness has produced the disappointment.

The third cause of lack of self-respect is a belief that failure deserves punishment. Bruce Narramore has underscored this, "We take in our parents' corrective attitude and actions just as we take in their goals, ideals, and expectations. To the degree our parents resorted to pressure, fear, shame, or guilt to motivate us, we developed a second false assumption. This is summed up in the thought, 'When I fall short of my goals or expectations, I need to be pressured, shamed, frightened, or punished.' "[7]

Self-punishment, like hostility toward others, is a violation of one of God's creations. Jesus was bruised for our iniquities, despised and rejected on our behalf. God takes no pleasure in our self-punishment, particularly when it means, as it usually does, that we are overlooking the importance of what Christ did for us. (Study Isaiah 53. It's exciting!) Self-punishment leads to self-pity which leads to more self-punishment which leads to lack of self-respect which leads us away from Jesus Christ who is the source of positive self-esteem.

Lack of self-respect causes us to deny even God's statements of our worth. Our confidence in our ability to make good choices or to do anything of significance is shattered. Feelings of insecurity are created, and we deny the expressions of love we need so much to hear.

Lack of Growth
A fourth hindrance to a positive self-concept is lack of growth. We accept and respect immaturity and physical limitations in children. However, when they become grownups we expect more

from them. Growth requires both food and water and is facilitated by regular exercise. In the spiritual and psychological areas this means healthy input from Scripture and from others, and the willingness to take risks. Chapter five, which emphasized learning to trust God, is intended to serve as a guideline for growth as a person of faith. Growth is not an option. It is a necessity. God is more interested in our growth than he is in our successes.

What happens when we do not grow? It is difficult to experience feelings of worth when there is no evidence of growth. What about confidence? Grown babies aren't confident. Security? When I feel that my growth has halted at an early stage of development, I am plagued by worry. Forty-year-old babies aren't secure. Lastly, if we haven't grown, accepting love is hard. Love based on acknowledged weakness is easy to accept when we are young, but when we are older that love loses its meaning. Failure to grow in the past does not mean that growth is impossible now. Some discipline will be necessary, though. Eat a balanced diet. Drink lots of good water and begin to exercise in all areas—physical, emotional and spiritual. Growth will soon follow.

Separated from God

The final hindrance to development of self-esteem is separation from God. God is not only the source of life; he is also the source of self-acceptance. Human acceptance is fickle and usually results in more questions about ourselves than answers. In contrast, God has repeatedly expressed his acceptance of us and has told us where we stand with him. Read carefully the words of David, "Praise the LORD, O my soul; all my inmost being, praise his holy name. Praise the LORD, O my soul, and forget not all his benefits. He forgives all my sins and heals all my diseases; he redeems my life from the pit and crowns me with love and compassion. He satisfies my desires with good things, so that my youth is renewed like the eagle's" (Ps 103:1-5). In the New Testament we find another word of assurance: "But these are written that you may believe that Jesus is the Christ, the Son of God, and that by believing you may have life in his name" (Jn 20:31).

Separation from God results from one of two conditions: never being connected with him or choosing to disconnect from God. The Bible clearly says that God stands ready to embrace any person who is willing to come to him. A vivid picture of this desire is presented in Matthew 11:28-30, "Come to me, all you who are weary and burdened, and I will give you rest. Take my yoke upon you and learn from me, for I am gentle and humble in heart, and you will find rest for your souls. For my yoke is easy and my burden is light." This acceptance is not based on our quality of life but on God's willingness to forgive us and to connect with us despite our sins. This accepting attitude also rings clear from Romans 5:8, "God demonstrates his own love for us in this: While we were still sinners, Christ died for us."

To solve the problem of never having been embraced by God, we merely need to request the relationship. Although this seems trite, becoming a child of God is easier than being connected with the electrical or telephone systems. The stumbling block is our unwillingness to submit to a higher power. Our pride often keeps us from saying yes. Pride makes the easiest thing in the world the hardest thing to do. Connecting with God is not cheap. Christ died to pay the hook-up fee, and now God is accessible to all on a free basis. The only cost to us is giving up trying to provide the power for ourselves. "For it is by grace you have been saved, through faith—and this not from yourselves, it is the gift of God —not by works, so that no one can boast" (Eph 2:8-9). To be connected with God in a personal way is the most exciting stimulant to self-worth that I can imagine.

Some who have connected with God have chosen for one reason or another to pull away from him. They believe in electricity, but they choose not to patronize the power company. They really do like being in the dark rather than the light. Unhooking from God may be just as devastating to self-acceptance as never connecting in the first place. To have a new Cadillac and yet drive the beat-up Chevrolet that doesn't even get better mileage isn't rational. Neither is refusing to follow God and deciding rather to practice self-defeating patterns of behavior.

We unhook from God for many reasons: fear, desire to pursue sin, indifference, anger, lack of understanding of what he wants to do for us. Whatever the reason, the result is the same. We will not reach the potential which the Creator intended for us. Frustration and sometimes anguish will follow.

Two stories from Scripture may be helpful to you if you are unhooked. The first is that of the wayward son recorded in Matthew 21:28-32. It shows us that God is always willing to reconnect us if we come home. A second story, the parable of the talents found in Matthew 25:24-30, reveals how we need to use our lives for God. If you have disconnected because of fear of God or because of an improper understanding of who God is, confess the sin and start over. God loves reclamation projects since they give him a chance to exercise his mercy and grace.

Regardless of the reason for being separated from God, all aspects of our positive self-image are affected. First, we are deprived of our greatest source of feelings of worth, the awareness that a perfect God accepts us even though we are imperfect. Second, we have no basis for confidence because we cannot rest until we find a resting place with the Creator. Third, we cannot experience security apart from being secure in our relationship with God. Last, we cannot know love if we refuse to be embraced by the essence of love.

Improper Labeling

Just knowing we have a problem is not enough. God is a God of solutions. In the next few pages we will focus our attention on ways that we can let God do his work.

First, we need to stop labeling as junk what God labels as valuable. Telling ourselves, others and God how bad we are never helps. God and others know how bad we are. That is not the point. The point is they choose to love us anyway. This is possible for God because Jesus paid for our badness. Others can love us because of the grace given them by God.

As a father, I am proud of my children. I don't call them names even though I realize that they have some defects. Furthermore, I don't let other people call them names. I respect them and I demand that they be respected. Lastly, I don't allow them to call themselves names. I do not have any "stupid" children. I only have children who, like their parents, may do stupid things.

Labeling, particularly negative labeling, is always risky, especially when we are disappointed with ourselves. God looked at his creation and saw that it was good. He also looks at his children and says, "I like you. You are mine."

Four Ways to Make the Cookie Crumble

Another way to allow God to help us with our self-esteem is to refuse to make crumbs. Making crumbs is a fine art form in which people take perfectly good compliments or positive feedback and quickly discredit it. If you received a cookie or a piece of cake from a friend and you crumbled it all up rather than enjoying it, that would be strange. If you did this too often, your friend might stop giving you the cookies because they are just wasted.

My friend Barbara, mentioned earlier in the chapter, had crumbmaking down to perfection. She received compliments because she was indeed attractive and gifted. But she never seemed to hear the compliments, so they gradually decreased. Even her husband grew weary of complimenting her. When I told her how lovely she looked, she crumbled the compliment by giving credit to an old dress. People make crumbs in many different ways. Let's look at some of the prominent areas.

First are the Prebake Crumbmakers. They always start the class, date, performance, game or even the fishing trip with a disclaimer. "I'm really not very good." "This isn't much." "The class won't be very good." "I haven't studied." "I didn't really have time to practice." This is a subtle form of the game Wooden Leg, discussed by Transactional Analysis creator, Eric Berne.[8] We play this game when we say, "Don't expect much of me because that's what you will get. Not much." Prebake Crumbmakers try to lower their anxiety by lowering expectations. Unfortunately, these statements often become a self-fulfilling prophecy since time and energy are drained off by the disclaimer. How much better it is when people pray, prepare, present, play, let God maximize the efforts, and praise him for enabling them to do a decent job! A little extra prayer never hurts.

In the second type of crumbmaking, Divide and Crumble, people give credit to everyone including the person who took out the garbage which left the room smelling better which made it easier to concentrate on the work. I am not trying to encourage ungratefulness. I too thank God for those who help me in so many ways. I am saying that it is not helpful if we divide and crumble and never acknowledge what God is doing through us. Accept praise from the coach and the spectators for your part on the team. Then give praise to God for the privilege of playing.

The third crumbmaker I call Susie Substitute. When complimented, Susie always says, "Yeah, but . . ." "Yeah, but you should hear my sister play. She's really good! She even played her own concert once." Susie, dear, you missed the point. I like the way you play. I appreciate the talent which God has given to you. I don't want a substitute. As neat as your sister may be, I don't care at this point. I enjoy hearing you play. I am thanking you for being who God made you to be and for using the talents God gave you to use.

The last group of crumbmakers are the most difficult to criticize because they hide in a blanket of religiosity. When complimented, such Christian Crumblers say, "It wasn't really me. It was the Lord." For example, John is a good pianist. When complimented he always has the same response. Raising his eyes toward heaven, he says, "It was just the Lord playing. It wasn't really me." The first time I heard this, I just passed it off. The second time he said it, I was miffed. "Knock it off, John!" I thought. "We both know the Lord can play better than that!"

Paul wrote in Galatians 6:4 that we are each to consider our own works, and then we will have reason to be proud. "Let every man learn to assess properly the value of his own work and he can then be rightly proud when he has done something worth doing, without depending on the approval of others" (Phillips). To consider our own works is to observe what God is enabling us to do. Pride is not a problem at this point. We are just being thankful for the tools God has given. Pride enters in when we feel we have to be the best to be worthwhile. Pride bursts in when we begin to compare ourselves with others.

Many Christians struggle for an appropriate response to compliments. May I suggest two words I have found helpful? "Thank you." We are never told in Scripture to guard our brothers and sisters against pride. God is uniquely capable of doing that. We are told to encourage one another and to challenge each other to love and good deeds. Don't make crumbs. That's a terrible waste.

God Reshaping
A third step in allowing God to improve our self-esteem is to begin to believe what God can do in us. I once wrote a professional manual which was well received and adopted at the state level. A Christian friend asked me how I could do that, given the fact that I had limited training in the area. As I tried to answer his question, I realized some things about the process. First, I believed that God could use my previous training even if it was not excessive. Second, I believed that God could quicken or sharpen my ideas. Third, I was willing to put forth the effort. And last, I was excited to see what kind of product God was going to enable me to produce. I was expecting good things from a good God. In the process there were times when I had to act "as if." As if I knew all the answers or, at least, as if I knew the right questions. I hope this was not arrogance. I worked hard to understand the problem I was writing about, and I took full advantage of both formal and informal consultants. In the final analysis, however, it was God and me. My work would be either accepted or rejected. Without faith it is impossible to please God, and I might add, without faith it is often impossible to accomplish anything. In this light I es-

pecially love the Old Testament name for God, El Shaddai, which emphasizes his might.

The crux of allowing God to develop our self-esteem is to believe that he wants to help us to be all we can be. Few people believe this emotionally. We "Yeah, but!" ourselves to death. God wants to shape and reshape us in an ongoing effort to conform us to the image of his Son (see Rom 8:29).

Understanding this analogy can be difficult because we live in a throw-away society. If something is marred, throw it out. This is not how God deals with us. He chooses to reshape us. In a real sense God can and does choose to turn sows' ears into silk purses. There is no greater stabilizer of self-esteem than to believe and act upon that fact by faith. This belief in the Potter who restores can do much to overcome the hindrances to a positive self-image. Placing ourselves in the hands of a God who delights in making beautiful things gives him the chance.

11
Choosing Emotions and Other Important Decisions

ONE OF THE MOST CONTROVERSIAL things I have said publicly during the last few years is that you can choose your emotions. This is hard for people to accept because we have been taught to believe that emotions are something that just happen to you. This is a stubborn belief because thinking that feelings just happen to me and that I am therefore not really responsible for them is quite comforting. Current theory of emotion, however, suggests that emotions are labels that we put on physiological reactions.

My father used to get angry when my mother cut herself. He would see blood and react. Why did he choose to get angry rather than show fear or sympathy? Was it a choice at all? I believe it was. There were times when I could see that he was about to express anger but would get control and say, "I'm really sorry this happened. Do you think it is going to be all right?" He probably showed anger at such times because that was how his father reacted. In other words how we express emotions can also be a habit learned by observing others. It is a habit which we can choose to try to break as my father did. Let's take another example.

Do you remember feeling threatened by a comment made by a stranger? How did you react? Did you retreat in fear? Did you strike out in anger? Did you wonder why this person, a stranger, would be hostile toward you? Did you feel any compassion? I suggest that you could have reacted in many different ways and that you could have chosen to have reacted differently. What are the areas of choice that we have when it comes to emotion?

First, we choose to label the internal stimulus as either a positive opportunity or negative problem. For example, the men Moses sent to spy out the land of Canaan all saw the abundance of the Lord. They brought back wonderful fruit. All of the spies also saw the giants who lived there. Some reported, "We seemed like grasshoppers in our own eyes, and we looked the same to them" (Num 13:33). Some said, "We can't attack those people; they are stronger than we are" (Num 13:31). In contrast, Caleb said, "We should go up and take possession of the land, for we can certainly do it" (Num 13:30). Caleb was physically aroused and had the same emotions as the others. I have little doubt that he was afraid. His faith, however, enabled him to make a difficult choice. He labeled the giants "conquerable."

During the time following physical arousal, which normally lasts four or five minutes, we also have an opportunity to choose our emotional response and the pattern of behavior we will follow. To be fearful is natural. This instinct keeps us alive. To choose to indulge fear, however, is never helpful. The Bible says, "Perfect love drives out fear" (1 Jn 4:18). I believe that this happens by choice. When something makes me afraid, I can choose to focus on the God who loves me rather than on what is causing the fear. Awareness of God's love then drives out fear. David wrote, "The LORD is the stronghold of my life—of whom shall I be afraid?" (Ps 27:1). I believe David was writing of choices he was making right at that time as he faced a frightening stimulus. Studies of stress conducted by Donald Meichenbaum and others have revealed that the patterns of thinking we employ and what we tell ourselves about a frightening stimulus allow us to choose panic or peace.[1] A woman forced to handle a snake was able to control her snake phobia by saying, "I'll make a deal with you, snake. You don't hurt me and I won't hurt you."

Now we are ready to answer the question, What does it mean to say that we can choose our emotions? We cannot choose what happens to us. God "sends rain on the just and on the unjust" (Mt 5:45 RSV). When an event (pleasant or unpleasant) happens, we go through two labeling processes. First we label the event as either good, bad or indifferent as discussed earlier. Second we label our body signal as fear, anger, happiness, grief, joy or the like. The labels we apply will come from our experience, but the label is not necessarily accurate. If we misjudge the situation, we need to correct it as soon as we become aware of it. The choices we make after the labeling process are therefore most critical. If we choose to emphasize the negative, fear or grief may turn into angry outbursts or uncontrolled crying. Unfortunately this happens frequently because we tend to act first and think the situation through after the damage has been done.

We might also choose to become either revengeful or forgiving if the stimulus involves another person. This type of choice is closely related to faith. It is difficult to make a choice to forgive unless we are trusting God to take care of us in the situation.

The Thoughtful Choice of Faith

If acting by faith in our choice of emotions is important, then such faith is also crucial in choosing our thoughts. The Scripture frequently refers to the need to control our thinking. I have already mentioned Paul's exhortation in Philippians 4:8 to focus our thoughts on what is true, noble, right, pure, lovely, admirable, excellent or praiseworthy. In 1 Timothy 4:16 he writes,

"Watch your life and doctrine closely," emphasizing the importance of right belief alongside right living.

The bottom line for Paul was choice, but choice based on as many facts as could possibly be gathered. This pattern of thinking-faith-choice is necessary if doubts are to be avoided. Guinness writes,

The issue at stake here is vital. If faith has nothing to do with knowledge, then we Christians doubt because our faith is weaker than knowledge. In this case our doubt would be only a local problem, a sign of the inferiority of our faith. It would be solved at once if we were to abandon faith for something more solid which can be known. On the other hand, if this distinction is wrong, if faith depends on knowledge and knowledge depends on faith, then doubt would be a challenge to both knowledge and faith and not just to faith.

In fact, the latter is the case. Without faith there is no knowledge. All true faith depends on knowledge. Knowledge and faith are inseparable.[2]

Knowing that faith must be applied to our thinking and thinking must be applied to our faith can help us understand what Hebrews means by "without faith it is impossible to please God." Choice is central to both. We choose to exercise faith, and we choose to exercise faith based on specific thoughts. Faith may be exercised without having all the facts. However, we must have some authority on which to rest our thought, faith and choice. I believe that the Bible provides us with reliable information about God and our world on which our choices in life can be confidently made.

Acting on Our Choice

People either choose to do what they want to do, what they feel they should do, what they think someone else wants them to do, what they are told to do, or else they try not to make any choice in the matter at all. Human behavior is just as confusing as thoughts and feelings. We say we want to do one thing but end up doing the other. We discipline ourselves to lose weight all week long only to splurge on the weekend.

The Epistle of James makes clear that faith must be expressed in behavior. "Someone will say, 'You have faith; I have deeds.' Show me your faith without deeds, and I will show you my faith by what I do. You believe that there is one God. Good! Even the demons believe that—and shudder" (Jas 2:18-19). Many problems can be traced to separating choosing from doing. These problems are so common that psychologists have studied several types of behavior that are affected.

The first type is called avoidance-avoidance. In such cases none of the options open to us look good. We feel we must act and others tell us we must act, but we are immobilized. Avoidance-avoidance conflicts can lead to high stress and crippling anxiety.

Faith may resolve these conflicts. Even if I don't like the thought of doing either thing, I can do one anyway if I have assurance that God is enabling me. Often as I face the issue and make a decision and do what I have been avoiding, I find that the situation is more tolerable than I had imagined. For example, I find it hard to be open with people. But when I trust God and take the risk, it usually isn't that bad.

The second type of choice problem is called approach-avoidance behavior. An apparent decision is made, but as the time to act approaches, negative feelings develop and we avoid the situation. Usually we feel guilty because we haven't met our overall goal.

My daughter Melissa wants to ride her horse instead of her pony. She says, "Dad, can I ride Sugar today?"

"Sure," I reply.

That night I notice that Sugar has not been ridden. When I ask her about it she says, "I just copped out, I guess!"

Technically she has become the victim of an approach-avoidance conflict. The closer she got to the goal, riding Sugar, the more fear and avoidance she felt.

In the spiritual realm we may decide to do something for God.

It may be to attend or lead a Bible study, or to talk to a friend about our own spiritual experience. As the opportunity for action approaches, however, we may find ourselves "copping out" and then even avoiding those who had encouraged us in our decision. Unable to apply faith to the choice, we fail to reach our stated goals.

A final type of conflict I call Second-Guessing Yourself. This results from the ambivalence we feel in many situations. We may choose a goal, but as we get close to that goal, we have both negative and positive thoughts or feelings.

I experience this every time I accept an invitation to speak at a conference. Initially I am excited about the opportunity, but as the day approaches I begin to wonder if I have adequately prepared. When I see the people arrive I feel excitement about the opportunity to meet them and share with them. But I also struggle with stage fright. What if my jokes are flat? What if my ideas are half-baked? What if my hair keeps falling in my eyes? I tell myself there are only one hundred people out there, but fear says, "Yeah, but there are two hundred eyes looking at you." Overcoming this ambivalence becomes a matter of faith. If I believe that God is with me then he can help me to overcome my fears and do what I have chosen to do. I can either second-guess myself or trust him to help me deal with my feelings of inadequacy.

In chapter four we saw that psychological dualism occurs when thinking and feeling do not converge in such a way that the choice results in a unified pattern of behavior. Let's examine the choice process more closely to see how we can make decisions to avoid that type of destructive dualism.

Psychologists who specialize in choice behavior view the decision-making process in phases. I use the following pattern:

1. Pinpoint the decision to be made.
2. Generate alternatives.
3. Evaluate and narrow the alternatives.
4. Select and act on the best alternative.
5. Re-evaluate the decision.

Each of these steps is necessary if decisions are to be made that result in unified behavior. We must remember, in addition, that any decision made by a believer is tied to faith. I either exercise faith in the decision-making process, or I choose to ignore God and try to make the choice alone.

Recently, Sandy and I were confronted with a serious problem which deeply affected both of us emotionally. She called to tell me about the problem at 7:00 A.M., and at 6:00 P.M. I was still struggling with the issues. As I was driving home, I realized I had spent the entire day ruminating over the problem and had not prayed about it at all. This was a danger signal to me because I believe it is essential to trust God to meet my needs if I am to maintain a balanced life. Prayer keeps me from distorting the data and is often used by God to bring my feelings and thinking together. Finally, prayer can also help me identify what is blocking unified action.

Let's examine the way faith is necessary at each phase of the choice process.

Pinpoint the Decision to Be Made

A common error in making choices is oversimplification. A seemingly straightforward decision such as whether or not to attend a party may, under closer scrutiny, prove to be quite complex.

That decision may involve a consideration of priorities in life if the party is scheduled the same evening as my Bible study. It may involve a consideration of values if I do not share the same lifestyle as others at the party. It may involve internal conflict if I am attracted to the party but also feel some avoidance. This approach-avoidance may be the beginning of dualism; that is, my feelings say, "Go for it," but my thinking says, "This is not who I want to be."

Any decision we make also affects future decisions. When trying to pinpoint decisions to be made, I ask myself two questions: What is the immediate decision? Does this decision have an effect on future decisions?

Jill went with Harry for two years before he broke off the relationship. Jill was deeply committed to Harry and was hurt badly by his decision. Harry said, "I just can't be tied down to one person. I have to have my freedom." Jill accepted the decision tearfully, not cheerfully, and tried to pull her life back together. She couldn't bring herself to date other people and soon Harry was back at her door. "I just can't live without you," he said. "However, I still can't give up my freedom." Jill was excited to have Harry back in spite of his second statement. Staying with Harry felt right because they had shared so many things together. She had felt almost married to him before he left. In fact, she felt guilty that the relationship hadn't worked.

Jill and Harry went out a few more times, and then Harry was gone again. As he had said, he just couldn't give up his freedom. This time Jill was not only hurt; she was confused and depressed. As we sorted through her feelings together, she got in touch with the fact that she saw Harry as her last hope. "After all," she said, "I'm twenty-five years old, and I don't meet many men that I like. Besides that, we had sex so I kind of feel like we are married. I don't know if anyone else would ever want me."

Jill was the victim of a nonmarriage marriage. Jill had made her commitment. She had given herself body and heart. Harry, on the other hand, had not given anything except some friendship and some good times. He had experienced the best that Jill had to offer. In fact, because of her marriagelike commitment to him, he could keep experiencing her best just as long as he dangled a carrot in front of her once in a while.

"Jill," I said, "nonmarriage marriages don't work. Harry is not capable of making a commitment to you."

She stubbornly resisted that thought while the tears streamed down her cheeks. "What can I do?" she cried.

"I don't know, Jill. I only know that a serious relationship without commitment is a dead-end street."

"But I've counted on this for so long," she sobbed. "I just can't start over."

Starting over is exactly what Jill had to do. We compared the dead-end street with a path out through the forest. Walking the dead-end street is easier. It's very familiar and comfortable. It feels right. But it just doesn't go anywhere! In contrast the path in the forest can be frightening. We can't tell where it leads. There isn't a familiar spot on it. It's all new.

"What if I walk out through the forest, and there is no one there for me?" she asked.

Her question was legitimate. I tried to be sensitive as I helped her understand that life has no guarantees. I was firm, however, as I said, "I know one thing; apart from a miracle there is no one for you on the dead-end street."

"I know that too," she said, "but I just can't accept it."

We talked about what going back to square one means. We worked through the question, "Is there life after twenty-five?" Jill said, "You know, I used to believe that God would provide a husband for me. I was such a romantic—white house, picket fence and all. When I met Harry I was so sure that he was the one that I guess I stopped trusting God. If I'm honest with myself, I think I probably had sex with him because way down inside I was afraid that I might lose him. Crazy," she said softly.

Jill had to consider whether or not she could trust God for her happiness and even trust him to provide her with a husband. The bottom line for Jill, as for you and me, is faith. Faith in a God who knows us and will meet our needs in singleness or in marriage. Spiritual and psychological dualism occurs when we stop believing that God will meet our needs and begin to take matters into our own hands, as Jill did. The decision which Jill had to pinpoint was much broader than whether or not to wait around for Harry. Hers was a decision of whether or not to trust God.

Generate Alternatives

When people come to me in distress, I find they often can't see different options. Bill is typical. "I can't think of anything I can do about it." After we talked for a while he began to loosen up and see that there were some choices available to him. "I guess I could drop some of my classes, but what about my plans? My parents will kill me if I don't get out of here in four years." Bill had never thought about talking to them. He had just assumed that they would be displeased and so threw the option out.

Bill's perfectionism also limited his options. He had to be the best, and when he found out that he wasn't, he became so upset that he was on the verge of being among the worst. He couldn't consider setting priorities for his studies to get A's in his most important classes so long as he demanded straight A's of himself. This led to inefficient study behavior and further confusion.

Another factor that limited Bill's ability to see alternatives was his feeling that God had abandoned him. He was dualistic. His thinking still believed, "God will never leave me nor forsake me," but his feelings believed, "I have been abandoned, and there is nothing I can do about it." God must weep at such self-imposed exile.

"Bill," I said, "you sure are in a pickle. It looks to me like you are going to have to trust God for something. What is it going to be?" With this new perspective Bill and I were able to brainstorm much more effectively, and he began to believe that with God's strength he would be able to work through his difficulties in school. When I picture Jesus standing at the door of the Christian's heart, knocking to gain entrance (see Rev 3:20), I picture him with bruised and bandaged knuckles. He has knocked on the door for so long he is about to wear out his hands, and we just keep ignoring the knock, choosing instead to focus on our distress.

Evaluate and Narrow the Alternatives

The third phase of choosing brings us face to face with our values. In trying to narrow the alternatives people ask one or more of the following questions: What do I want? What do my family or friends want me to do? What does God want me to do? These questions all concern values and expectations.

A parallel set of questions deals with another important aspect of narrowing alternatives—capability: What talents or abilities do I have? What do other people think I can do well? What has God gifted me to do?

A third set of questions concern long-range plans: How will each alternative open to me affect my long-range goals? Is the decision reversible, or will it cause other options to be closed in the future? Narrowing alternatives without closing down future options is most difficult. Sometimes it is impossible. You can't decide to have sex today and be a virgin tomorrow. On the other hand, a decision to go to one university does not preclude later attending another.

Applying faith to the narrowing alternatives is difficult because we "can't have our cake and eat it too." On the other hand, God delights in giving good gifts to his children (Mt 7:11). When, in faith, we narrow alternatives, we are in effect saying, "God, I believe that if I follow this path I will find you there, going before me. You will meet me whichever path I take, but I believe this is the path best suited for me now."

Select and Act on the Best Alternative

The words of Jesus quoted above emphasize the need for action to follow choice. There is a time for making a decision and a time for acting on that decision. Faith at this point says, "God, I will trust you for whatever is needed to do what I feel you are leading me to do." God gives us enough time each day to do all the things he wants us to do. If you have more than you can do, he may be telling you to choose to do less.

It was extremely difficult for me to decide to turn down one-time speaking engagements that emphasize evangelism. I do not have the gift of evangelism although I try to live an evangelistic lifestyle. I have the gift of teaching and am most effective when I work with people over a period of time. I was being overrun by requests to speak for thirty minutes here and thirty minutes there. God had to show me that other people could do that better and that I needed to concentrate on other opportunities. Acting on that decision was difficult. I had to say no! John Alexander, president emeritus of Inter-Varsity Christian Fellowship, once stated at a faculty conference I attended, "You will never be a mature Christian until you learn to say no." If you say yes under God's guidance, then do it! If you are led to say no, then don't hang your head. God has something else for you to do.

Re-evaluate the Decision

The final phase in making God-directed choices is periodic re-evaluation and reinforcement of those decisions which were particularly helpful to you. You will make mistakes. Don't spend time berating yourself for those. Just learn from them and try to make wiser decisions in the future. As you identify good choices you have made, remind yourself to take advantage of similar opportunities in the future. God will use this to maximize your God-given potential.

The wise counsel of a friend can also help. Often such a friend can look at your choices and evaluate them without the emotional investment which you might have. Dave said to me, "I think you could use your time more wisely by doing more teaching and less administration." I didn't like that because I like to think that I can do both. I followed his suggestions, however, and have been blessed by God because of that. Thanks, Dave.

Nonchoice Choices

I would be remiss in writing a chapter on faith and choices without discussing one important problem area, the problem of nonchoice choosing. I sometimes call this invisible choices. At an Inter-Varsity chapter meeting where I spoke, I overheard Jim and Tom talking.

"How did you decide to ask Becky out, Tom?" Jim asked.

"I don't know," Tom answered. "It just happened. We were together a lot, so it just happened, I guess."

In this case the consequences of an invisible choice were not so bad. Tom and Becky enjoy each other and although they will probably never have a serious relationship, they will help each to grow as people. If, however, either of them had been a different type of person, this nonchoice choice could have been harmful to one or both.

As a marriage counselor, I have been appalled at the number of young Christians who get married not by choice but by nonchoice. They never decided not to marry, so they ended up married and, in many cases, miserable.

I believe Jesus wants us to live active, decisive lives. Choose whom you will marry. Decide what values you want to cultivate in your life. People who go through life only reacting, never acting on their own feelings and thoughts, become fragmented people. There are times when discretion tells us to wait and watch, but in general we need to ask God to help us plot a course for our lives and then live out that course. Maybe that's what Paul meant when he said, "Therefore, my dear friends, as you have always obeyed—not only in my presence, but now much more in my absence—continue to work out your salvation with fear and trembling, for it is God who works in you to will and to act according to his good purpose" (Phil 2:12-13).

The missing element in nonchoice choices seems to be commitment. I don't choose because I am afraid to commit myself to a plan of action. I often can't choose because I lack the faith to believe God will be with me in my choice. This problem has been enlarged by a current ethic which says, "If it feels good, do it." The problem is I can't even choose what feels good because the moment I choose, something else may come along that feels better.

When Sandy and I worked with the singles group at our church, we invited them to come to our house for Christmas dinner. We were amazed that no one jumped at the chance even though many were away from their families. As it turned out a few called the last minute when they were sure they weren't going to get a better offer. (A better offer in this case would probably mean an invitation from a male or female friend.) Some of them failed to make any commitment, were ashamed to call at the last minute and ended up spending Christmas day alone in their apartments. They didn't choose isolation. That was an invisible choice.

Focusing Our Choices

Everett Worthington has pointed out that we need to strive not only for consistency in our lives but also for lives governed by God's will. In figure 9 he focuses our attention on making choices which align us with the will of God. We choose feelings which are consistent with God's will. We choose thoughts which are consistent with his will. We choose to act consistently with his will. We even choose to make choices which bring us in line with God's purposes.

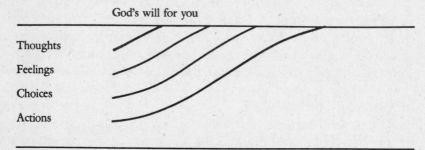

Figure 9   Choosing to Line Up with God

We have seen then that faith and choice interact with our feelings, our thoughts and our actions. Choice is a process that each of us needs to learn. If we don't learn to make decisions, we may end up living our entire lives with nonchoices. But choices made on the basis of faith in God hold our lives together.

12
Resolving Responsibility

AS A PARENT I HAVE COME to hate one simple phrase, "It's not my fault." Invariably this comes up when emotions are disturbed. "It's not my fault. I'm upset. I didn't do anything. Don't blame me." Accepting or refusing to accept responsibility for our actions is a key to integrating our choosing with the other aspects of our lives. Denial of blame and refusal to accept the consequences, to own responsibility for our behavior, are problems that are as old as mankind. Adam used it and so did Eve.

Confusion about blame also occurs when we experience some emotional pain. A boyfriend breaks off our relationship. My father is in a car accident. I find out a neighbor has lied to me. At such times, we become plagued by two nagging questions: "Why?" and, "Whose fault is it?" Depending on how the questions are answered, the two may blend together to become a strong block against a sense of personal worth. If the answer to "Why?" is "Because I'm bad," then the pain is obviously my fault. In similar fashion if we believe it is our fault, we will tend to see the focus of the pain as punishment.

Recently an unwed expectant mother sat nervously in my office trying to muster the spiritual and emotional strength to continue with life. In desperation she said, "I think I could go on if I just knew why. God must have a purpose," she sighed.

"LuAnn," I said, "you are pregnant because you had sexual intercourse. You disobeyed one of God's commandments, and you are experiencing the results of one of God's natural laws. When an ovum and a sperm are united a new life is formed. The question is not why did God do it or even why did God allow it. The question is, How are you going to respond now, and what can you expect from God at this point? God may choose to use your experience in some special way or he may not. One thing you can be sure of, however, is that he loves you and will be with you in the midst of your struggle."

Initially LuAnn didn't like what I had to say. I was forcing her to accept responsibility for her actions. "It would be easier," she said, "if I thought I was just a pawn in God's mysterious and marvelous plan." I encouraged her to accept responsibility for her behavior and for the new life within her. We began a tedious but worthwhile process of sorting out responsibility, of owning sin and mistakes while at the same time learning not to take responsibility that was not hers. She needed to know that the baby's father was also responsible.

Sponges and Squeegees

Biologists and psychologists have long recognized that people have a strong need to maintain equilibrium. When an intrusion occurs, whether physical or mental, we go to great lengths to regain the status quo. We try, sometimes desperately, to get back to normal or to put things in their place.

Emotional pain is such an intrusion. It causes us uncertainty and unrest. If love has been withdrawn in a relationship, you may amaze yourself by all you will do to regain that love or to prove to yourself that you are still lovable. This often results in mistake being heaped on mistake until a situation becomes intolerable. Assigning responsibility is one of the mechanisms often used to regain emotional balance.

Think of responsibility as a puddle in the middle of the floor. We are uncomfortable by the unsightly mess. Our tendency toward equilibrium unconsciously or consciously reacts. "Whose fault is it?" we ask. The puddle must be cleaned up. Some respond like a sponge—they throw themselves into the puddle, seeking to soak up all the guilt before others notice it or even before they have evaluated the source of the problem.

Sheri is a sponge. Any time something goes wrong she is quick to say, "It's all my fault." She can't stand the tension of unresolved conflict. "I learned that from my father." she reported. "Any time he would even raise his eyebrows at me I would say how sorry I was that he was upset, even if I didn't know why." Sheri never got close to her father because they didn't have an honest relationship. In fact, people who are sponges wanting to slurp up blame often develop unconscious resentments which hinder their emotional growth and prevent close relationships.

Others respond to the puddle like a squeegee. They push or pull the water of responsibility, never accepting it as their own. Quickly and thoroughly, they manage to remove the water from the neutral area and soak others with the uncomfortable moisture and stains.

Bill is a squeegee. He can clean up any sticky situation without getting a drop on himself. Bill can be quite loud and cutting in his speech. He doesn't notice the way that his brashness affects other people. When they retreat from him because of hurt feelings or when they counterattack, his response is predictable. "What did I do? What's wrong with her? I didn't say anything!" People who know Bill just shake their heads. People who might want to know him decide there are better alternatives. Bill says, "It's not my fault I don't have friends. People just don't seem to have time for me."

Accepting responsibility appropriately may be the ultimate in living a life balanced among thinking, feeling, choosing and doing. Figure 10 shows the function of each area as it relates to the acceptance of responsibility.

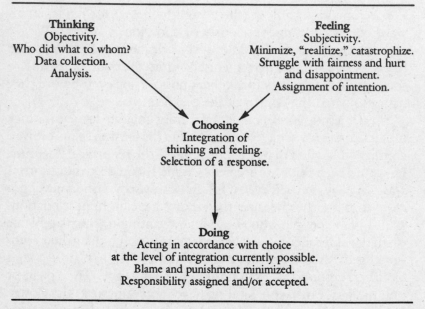

Thinking
Objectivity.
Who did what to whom?
Data collection.
Analysis.

Feeling
Subjectivity.
Minimize, "realitize," catastrophize.
Struggle with fairness and hurt
and disappointment.
Assignment of intention.

Choosing
Integration of
thinking and feeling.
Selection of a response.

Doing
Acting in accordance with choice
at the level of integration currently possible.
Blame and punishment minimized.
Responsibility assigned and/or accepted.

Figure 10   Functional Evaluation of Responsibility

Ideally our thinking serves as the data collector when we want to assign responsibility. The questions are first *what* and then *who*. What are the facts of the matter? Objectivity breaks down when our thinking is bombarded with our feelings or when it attempts to resolve issues of fairness or to ascertain why certain things happened.

Feelings are important in resolving responsibility because unless feelings are considered, the issue of responsibility will never be resolved. We must keep in mind that feelings are real and must be considered, but they are not necessarily based on truth.

A Case Study: Spilled Milk
Consider the case of the spilled milk. As one family, that shall remain anonymous, gathered at the table for the evening meal, Mother (hereafter referred to as P1) asked Father (P2) to pour the milk for the children (c1, c2, c3, c4 and c5). P2 carried out his duties carefully and finished the task with a firm reminder, "Be careful now. I filled those glasses pretty full. We don't want any milk spilled."

The family sits down. P2 asks c3 to say grace which he does but only after asking, "Is it my turn again? You always ask me to pray."

C3 says, "Amen and pass the potatoes," and at the same time a glass of milk bites the dust.

P2, calm as usual, yells, "Who spilled the milk? I told you to be careful!"

P1 says, "What a mess! And I just washed this kitchen floor!"

C1, c2 and c3 all say, "I didn't do it," and breathe a sigh of relief.

C4 and c5 each point to the other and say, "It wasn't my milk."

C3 repeats his demand for the potatoes and reaches for the meat. C1 and c2, both teen-agers, smugly watch P1 and P2 as if to say, "Let's see how you handle this one."

P2 continues to exhibit his brilliance by screaming, "Why can't you kids be more careful?"

P1 says, "Don't just sit there. Get a rag and clean it up. Oh, what a mess!"

C1, a female of the species, notices the tears in the eyes of c4 and c5 and comes to the rescue. "I'll clean it up," she says. C2 is almost as helpful. He reminds the family that they are supposed to leave in fifteen minutes and that they haven't even eaten yet.

P2, angered by what he considers less than constructive comments from c2, reaches to pass the salad and in the process knocks over his own glass of water.

c_1, c_2, c_3, c_4, c_5 and P_1 are all strongly silent, holding back their laughter. P_2 joins them in stunned silence.

c_5, too young to know better, breaks in by saying, "Dad, you filled the glasses too full."

P_2 responds by saying, "Okay, Okay!! I spilled my water. What I want to know is who spilled the milk?"

c_4 and c_5 once again point to each other. c_4 says, "We both did it. It was right in the way. It was an accident."

P_2 looks angry and annoyed. He speaks, "Yeah! I suppose it's the cow's fault. She should never have given the milk."

c_3 seizes the opportunity. "Let's blame God," he says. "He made the cows."

P_1 comes to the rescue. "c_4 and c_5," she asks, "who knocked over the glass of milk?"

"We both hit it," they reply.

c_4, looking sheepish, adds, "I guess I was trying to beat c_3 to the potatoes."

P_1 says, "Okay! For whatever reason, you two spilled the milk. You may scrub the floor after supper. That will help you remember to slow down."

P_2 says, "I think I better help. I got too excited and wasn't careful either."

c_4 says, "Maybe God could do the waxing."

"Maybe God could pass the potatoes," retorts c_3. The family relaxes but only for a moment.

"Oh, my goodness!" exclaims c_1. "It's almost time to go. You know I hate being late!"

What are the facts of the case? If we stop to think through the situation we will see: (1) the milk was spilled jointly by c_4 and c_5; (2) P_2 spilled the water; (3) c_3 or, for that matter, all the other family members may have been controlling factors, but they did not spill anything—this time; (4) there is no evidence that anyone intended to hurt anyone else or that they were even being overly reckless; (5) charges must be dismissed against both the cow and God.

Now let's get subjective. What sorts of feelings were entertained? P2: disgust, anger and indignation because his caution was not taken seriously; guilt and humiliation came later as he became part of the problem rather than the solution. P1: frustration and disappointment because of the floor and the confusion; amazement and amusement over P2's lack of control. C1 and c2: lack of involvement and glee in being spectators. C3: defensiveness and then awareness that his impatience may have been a contributing factor. C4 and c5: defensiveness, fear, projection of blame on others and, finally, owning responsibility.

When each person acknowledged the facts that people, not God, caused the problem, it was easier to accept their feelings and integrate them into the total picture. Sorting out contributing factors before the primary factors (I knocked over the glass) are acknowledged is usually not helpful. Each person should strive to deal with his or her own actions; that is, what did I do? I knocked over the glass. What do I do now? Clean up the mess.

When this response pattern is followed, problems of character assassination are avoided. P1 did not say, "You are a bad person." She said, "C4 and c5, you spilled the milk." Inducing guilt is a poor substitute for calling for responsible action ("You may scrub the floor"). Each person, including P2, was able to accept (choose) responsibility without continuing to blame or punish either self or others.

Galatians 6:4 reminds us that each of us must carry his or her own load. This means we must bear the responsibility for our own actions. Note that blame and punishment are often a part of the process of sorting out responsibility. This can usually be set aside when responsibility for the action and for the contributing factors is accepted. Quickly soaking up all the blame like the sponge or passing it on to the other person like the squeegee is not constructive. God wants us to own the part that is ours.

Responsibility in Relationships

I spend a great deal of my professional time helping people sort through responsibility issues related to broken relationships. College students struggle when their parents' divorce. They sometimes feel the problems are their fault. Married couples experience the intrusion of an extramarital affair and wonder who is responsible for the breakdown. Engaged couples break up and wonder whose fault it is.

Often the facts need to be faced, such as lack of compatibility. Both are equally responsible. When there is adultery, each person should face the question of who committed the infidelity. We are each responsible for our own acts. If you are a contributing factor, you may wish to consider how you could be helpful rather than hurtful. But accepting responsibility for the acts of the other person only muddies the waters.

Mrs. Markum was shattered when her husband told her he had had an affair. This hooked her feelings of inadequacy. She went back and forth between blaming him and blaming herself.

I asked, "Who had intercourse outside the marriage?"

Faintly she said, "Well, he did." She sat for a moment, then more strongly said, "If I hadn't had that mastectomy . . . " She was willing to blame herself, if necessary, in order to resolve the question, "How could he do this?" or the deeper question, "How could he do this *to me?*"

"He did this to you because he is sinful," I said. "He made a stupid decision, and you are trying to justify it for him by accepting responsibility when you did not violate your marriage vows. He did!"

I retraced this ground several times with Mrs. Markum. She agonized as the very roots of her self-acceptance were being shaken, even though, at the same time, she was struggling with feelings of revenge.

She returned often to her problem with body image. "Mrs. Markum," I said, "If you had the body of one of Charlie's Angels and the disposition of one of God's angels, your husband would still have made this bad choice. He had an affair because he was consumed by his lust, not because you are inadequate."

Somehow we have come to believe that if someone is hurt or sinned against, they must bear some responsibility for the offender's sin. We tend to allow the offender to be seen as innocent and to see the "innocent party" as responsible. We say, "If I were a better person, this wouldn't have happened to me." Of others we say, "If he hadn't spent so much time at work, she wouldn't have had the affair." These are not true statements; they are assumptions which are usually incorrect. Even "perfect" people get hurt.

This thinking is fruitless. It leads to dualism rather than resolution of responsibility. We end up hating ourselves and the other person, without being able to forgive either. Mrs. Markum could not forgive herself or her husband so long as she kept going back and forth between blaming him and blaming herself. Once she was able to leave the responsibility for her husband's adulterous behavior with him, she could forgive and then turn her emotional energies to the question, What kind of wife do I want to be? How can I better meet his needs? Through this process she may discover some sin for which she needs to ask forgiveness, but she must not accept the responsibility for the sin of her husband.

The account of Jesus and the Samaritan woman found in John 4 demonstrates the straightforward way in which Jesus led her to accept responsibility for her sinful behavior and then to move on to a better way of living. You may recall that they met at a well where Jesus began telling the woman about a water that would quench her thirst forever. Then, seemingly abruptly, he changes the topic.

"Go, call your husband and come back."

"I have no husband," she replied.

Jesus said to her, "You are right when you say you have no husband. The fact is, you have had five husbands, and the man you now have is not your husband. What you have just said is quite true."

"Sir," the woman said, "I can see that you are a prophet. . . ."

Then, leaving her water jar, the woman went back to the

town and said to the people, "Come, see a man who told me everything I ever did. Could this be the Christ?" (Jn 4:16-19, 28-29)

Jesus did not condemn or patronize her. He was factual, and the woman was able to respond by accepting responsibility for her sin, by accepting Christ as the Messiah and, undoubtedly, by accepting herself.

Mrs. Markum tried to resolve responsibility by being a sponge. John was a squeegee. But the results were just as negative. He was eighteen and in the middle of his first semester at the university. Frankly, he was not doing well. He hadn't cracked a book for two weeks and was beginning to show some of the early signs of fear of failure. I asked him how he liked college.

"Oh, fine! The people are really neat!"

"How are the studies going?" I asked.

"Okay, I guess," he said quizzically. "College is sure a lot more Mickey Mouse than I expected."

I just smiled and said, "I'm listening." He began to unload.

"Those assignments are crazy. You have to read hundreds of pages and it doesn't make any sense. I don't know where most of my professors are headed. They're just stupid."

The more he talked, the more agitated he became. The more agitated he grew, the more he blamed others. He was gripped by the fear of his own failure but didn't have a way to deal with it except to squeegee the responsibility on someone else. After a long time of listening and trying to hear where he was hurting, I decided to try to lead him out of the trap he was setting for himself.

"John," I said, "let's assume that everything you have told me is true. College is kind of dumb and the professors really are insensitive. They overload you, and they aren't accessible when you get confused about an assignment. I'd recommend that you drop out of school. Why subject yourself to this kind of mental torture when there is absolutely nothing you can do to change the outcome? It's obvious from what you told me that even if you studied day and night, and even if you cut out all your social life and stopped working, you couldn't make it. This is a loused-up situation and system."

John got my message and began to be more honest. "I really haven't used the study time I have," he said. "I've been so angry I haven't even been willing to try to study. I might be able to make it, but I have to get a better attitude. I think my head is as messed up as some of my professors."

Once I got John to put away his squeegee, he was able to make some responsible choices, accept responsibility for himself and do what needed to be done. He began to rescue his faltering college career.

Blocks to Resolving Responsibility
Let's look more closely at how trying to resolve issues of responsibility may lead to psychological dualism. When responsibility has not been assigned, we tend to vacillate between two sets of actions. One minute we blame ourselves. The next minute we blame the other person. Rarely are we able to take any constructive action until we can resolve the issue and be single-minded. It's like not being able to serve both God and mammon. What keys will unlock this jail? A number of factors block the integration of thinking and feeling at the level of choice when dealing with responsibility.

The first is the quest for simple solutions. I become concerned when I hear someone say, "It's easy. Just don't think about it," or, "It's simple. Just trust God." As I pointed out in chapter five, trusting God is not simple, neither are sorting out responsibility and putting together facts and feelings. Sometimes our feelings even distort the facts. Sometimes we are afraid to consider the facts because they may hurt too much or may cause us to act in a way our feelings don't like.

Second, and closely related to the quick, simple solutions, is our inability to handle ambivalence. We like to feel that things are all settled. When sin entered the world, it distorted the stability of life. Thus, ambivalence developed over many areas of life. Adam and Eve, for example, were not ambivalent about their sexuality until after the Fall. Then they began to cover up. Before that they were not ashamed. Many relationships today are love-hate relationships. In fact, most of us even love and hate ourselves. In trying to assign responsibility we would like to do away with this ambivalence, but we can't. So dualism often results.

Jennifer and Bill are having difficulty. Bill has trouble accepting Jennifer's past and therefore acts inconsistently toward her. Sometimes he is affectionate; sometimes he is distant. The wear and tear on both of them is beginning to show. Jennifer's feelings often focus on regret over her past; "If only I hadn't . . . !" Her thinking says, "But I'm not that way now! That was long ago." She does just fine when Bill is constantly attentive but gets into trouble when he can't maintain that warmth. When Bill is down, Jennifer accepts the responsibility at the feeling level but doesn't let the facts speak. If Jennifer and Bill do not accept the ambivalence of the situation, their severe pain will continue and will destroy their relationship regardless of whether or not they get married.

The ambivalence Bill must face is this: Jennifer loves me and is committed to me even though I am not the only love she has known; I regret the fact that I cannot be the one and only, but that does not mean that Jennifer cannot be my true love right now. Jennifer's ambivalence is similar: Bill loves me and is committed to me, but he is struggling; some days he cannot reach out to me; I have to let that be his problem so that I can receive his love and affection when it is expressed; his ups and downs do not mean that we cannot meet each other's needs right now. Resolving ambivalence requires that each person accept his or her own responsibility without accepting responsibility for the behavior of the other person.

A third block to resolving responsibility is uncontrolled thinking that leads to catastrophizing. This in turn can cause emotional upset. When Bill is down, he tells himself how awful it is that Jennifer is not a virgin. "I can't stand it!" he cries within himself. "How could she do this to me?"

While counseling him, I said, "Tell me, Bill, how she did this to you. She must have said, 'I'll show Bill. I'll have sex with Richard and that way Bill can never be happy!' "

Bill's anguish was obvious. He put his head in his hands and said, "No! No! She didn't even know me then. I don't mean to do this to her."

"She'll survive, Bill! Will you?" I replied.

The bottom line for Bill is this: he does not have to like the fact that Jennifer had a life before meeting him. It's O.K. to have regrets. Jennifer also has some of those. However, Bill must stop telling himself that because of that past he cannot be happy and that he must continue to hold himself and Jennifer accountable. In other words, Bill needs to deal with reality and let the past be past so that he can enjoy the beauty of his relationship with Jennifer right now.

Fourth, a related block is the tendency to distort facts. There are two common errors in this regard: misperceiving the facts or trying to establish generalizations. We know the story of the three blind men who each described the elephant in a different way because they each felt a different part of the elephant. What is harder to realize is that sighted people may also see facts differently or choose to emphasize diffcrent facts.

John, the college freshman with the squeegee, initially perceived his problem as stemming from the erratic behavior or the excessive assignments of the professor. Questions allowed him to discover his misperception. His misperceptions were corrected by self-discovery. (The Socratic method works best in cases like this because we can't argue people into seeing things as we see them.) They will cling to a private set of facts just as the blind person describes the elephant only in terms of the trunk which he has touched.)

Misperceptions related to intention often occur because we believe that other people have the same motives we have. If you are vindictive, you will probably attribute vindictiveness to the other. We may, however, at times attribute opposite motives to others. In either case, misperceptions occur and integration is blocked.

Faulty generalization results when we see two situations to be alike even though they are not. When we make faulty generalizations, we might end up making wrong choices. Ruth trusts men because she trusted her father. She therefore interprets the behavior of her boyfriend John from this perspective. If she is taken advantage of in her relationship with John she may say, "He is trustworthy; it's all my fault." When this faulty generalization occurs, integration will be blocked because she can't match her thoughts and feelings.

In such situations we need a friend to point out how the two situations or people differ. As we are able to identify these differences, we can accept one person's negative behavior without needing to change our positive perception of the other. We can also ask ourselves such questions as, Are these people alike? How are the two situations different? What might I do to discover whether or not the same rules apply here as there?

A fifth factor which blocks integration is unresolved anger. I once participated in a debate on the University of Nebraska-Lincoln campus in which the topic was premarital sex: pro and con. The person who set up the debate tried to stack the cards and expected the students to go away "liberated from some of their guilt over promiscuous behavior." In my own trembling, earthy fashion, I brought up emotional issues the students could identify with—being used, mutual masturbation, loss of identity and the hollowness of pleasure without a relationship. I'm sure I didn't win the debate technically. But people did resonate with what I had to say. I left them struggling with a haunting awareness that I might be right and the biblical position just might not be as far off base as my opponent was leading them to believe.

As I was about to leave, the organizer of the debate approached me. "I need to talk to you," he said.

"Great," I replied. "These issues are always of interest to me."

"I don't want to talk about issues," he replied. "I want to shout at you."

He was probably dealing with some unresolved responsibility. His objectives, public or private, for the debate had not been met. He probably blamed me outwardly and himself inwardly. Until he resolved the anger, he could not bring his thoughts and feelings together.

Resolution of anger also requires a choice. We need to choose either not to be upset by the events or to choose to release the anger through forgiveness. My friend did not have to like my part in the debate. But he needed to choose not to be immobilized by either my actions or the outcome of the debate since he could not forgive me at that time.

Hollow Forgiveness

This leads us to a sixth block to integration—meaningless forgiveness. I am always alarmed when I hear someone say, "Oh, I forgive her! I just forgive everyone. This is what Jesus wants me to do." Forgiveness without adequate assessment of the offense is hollow forgiveness. You can only really forgive after you have evaluated the extent of the damage. When God forgives us for our sins, he does so with full awareness of their awfulness. Our sins are so bad, in fact, that they required an awesome penalty—death, the death of God's Son on our behalf. True forgiveness costs.

One day as I came down the stairs I heard a series of crashes. I could detect the sound of shattering glass. I rushed to the family room, and there were my three oldest children peering sadly at the remains of some items that we had brought back from our year in Iran. I was angry. I bawled them out severely. Finally, the tirade ended, I sent them to their rooms with a glib statement that they were forgiven.

Later as I picked up the pieces of all my memorabilia I was overtaken by external sadness. These things which had high significance to me had been destroyed by the carelessness of my children. I even wept as I realized that they could never be replaced. I fought off the urge to call them back into the room and punish them again. Later I was able to realize that I had not really forgiven them because at the time of my glib statement I hadn't even realized all they had done. I was then able to go to them and say, "You have broken things that meant a lot to me, but you mean too much to me to let that stay between us. I *do* forgive you."

Unless this type of forgiveness occurs, there will continue to be blocks to integration. In *Caring Enough Not to Forgive,* which is the flip side of his book *Caring Enough to Forgive,* Augsburger relates a personal experience which can direct us out of the trap of meaningless forgiveness.

"Forget it, it didn't matter at all, it was nothing," I once said to a man who wanted to work through a past difficulty with me. On later reflection I discovered I had some feelings about his stiff words that I had closed off somewhere inside myself. "Why feel hurt about his insensitivity, he wasn't that important to me," I had decided deep within. Unfair. Untrue. And his coming back to initiate reconciliation had punched a hole in the wall of my internal isolation process; so finally recognizing the reality within, I could call him back. "I'm discovering I do have some feelings after all, let's talk."[1]

A seventh block is fear. Fear can stop you short in thinking, feeling, choosing and doing. Fear that blocks the input from our thinking is particularly devastating. We are warned against anxiety by Scripture. "Do not be anxious about anything, but in everything, by prayer and petition, with thanksgiving, present your requests to God" (Phil 4:6).

Fear blocks integration in several ways. Our fear of negative evaluation by others often results in procrastination. We even procrastinate about deciding whether or not to put things off. Fear can also prevent us from setting guidelines by which we can move forward to resolve ambivalence. We suffer from fear of failure, fear of rejection, fear of ridicule and even a more encompassing fear of intimacy. These keep us from getting new facts which will help us accept responsibility that is ours and let go of responsibility that is not ours. In other words, to be freed from the anxiety of accepting responsibility, we must take risks. Hauck writes,

Unless you are willing to take a chance and to expose yourself to the very thing that you are most afraid of, you have very little chance of ever overcoming your fear. You overcome a fear because you do the thing you are afraid to do and are willing to face the dangers involved. It does not matter whether you are climbing mountains or standing up to your boss, the principle is always the same: to overcome the fear, you must take certain risks. Those persons who do not take risks live in a constant state of anxiety and apprehension.[2]

When Sandy, my wife, began to write her story of God's love for her, she was afraid to put things down on paper. "What if it doesn't say what I want to say?" she asked. I encouraged her to write first and critique later. In other words, take the challenge. Face the fear and make adjustments as they seem appropriate. When you find yourself out of balance because of fears, you need to confront those fears before they become a way of life. Philippians 4:6, cited above, stresses the need to involve God in the solution.

This brings us to the eighth and final block to resolving dualism. We leave God out of the equation. Day by day as I talk to people about the problems they are facing, I find that when the going gets rough, they try to find a solution without God's help. "I just quit praying. I don't read my Bible anymore. I can't bring myself to go to church. I feel like too much of a failure to go to God." This list could be greatly expanded.

When I first saw Mary, she was suffering from extreme agoraphobia, a fear of being alone or of being caught in a public place with no escape from danger. She could hardly stand to be out of sight of her husband; therefore, she couldn't do the things she wanted or needed to do. She went to church once in a while when her fears would allow her to do so, but in general she grew more and more internal, more and more unstable, and she was having an increasing number of immobilizing attacks. She couldn't pray and the Bible was a closed book.

As I worked with Mary I forced her to face her fears and to begin to see that God was with her during those fearful times. She developed new emotional and spiritual muscles as I forced her to rely on her own muscle—not just on her husband. She began to see her own growth and to feel that God loves her and is with her even when she is panicked.

Recently I saw another exciting change. Mary has begun to take risks without my having to assign them, just because she wants to see God work. When I last talked to her husband, he said, "It's a miracle. She does things on her own, and she hasn't yelled in weeks. She is reading the Bible and praying, and I am too." This family has put God back into the equation and the results are obvious to those who see them. Mary doesn't look or act like an old person anymore. She is alive in Christ.

Accepting appropriate responsibility requires us to use both our thinking and our feelings. Evaluate your life to see what blocks you from integrating your thinking and feeling into unified choices and behavior. Searching for simple solutions, not living with ambivalence, catastrophizing thoughts, distorting facts, not resolving anger, offering meaningless forgiveness, being controlled by fear and leaving God out of the equation are all possible. Faith that holds together trusts God to help us accept responsibility for our sin and to forgive those who sin against us.

13
Faith in Action: The Joy of Doing

FRIEDRICH NIETZSCHE MADE the provocative statement, "There was only one Christian and he died on the cross." This is a stinging indictment against a Christianity that doesn't do anything. The ministry of Christ, short as it was, touched thousands within three years without the benefit of modern media. Jesus was truly an example of faith in action. Even at age twelve, when he stayed behind in the Temple, he told his parents, "Why were you searching for me?. . . Didn't you know I had to be in my Father's house?" (Lk 2:49). Jesus had a sense of purpose. He knew what he was about. He was a doer.

After I have failed I am tempted to rationalize by comparing myself to Jesus. "But he was the God-man. Things were easier for him." Then I think of the rejections he felt, the agony of Gethsemane and the cross, and I must stop kidding myself. He was a purposeful man of action, and he wants me to emulate this. Why is it that our best efforts often fall so short? What problems do we face in trying to apply faith to our doing? Let's consider three areas.

1. *Faith to choose to do the right thing.* There are many people who do and do and do and yet never do the things they feel they should do. They read James 2:14, "What good is it, my brothers, if a man claims to have faith but has no deeds? Can such faith save him?"—but seemingly to no avail. First of all their problem is a need to choose the most desirable action. It takes faith to follow through on our choices and do what we know we should. If this is your struggle, ask God to help you follow through on something today, a little thing, anything. There is no substitute for the joy of doing. Constructive, purposeful action which flows out of God's will for you will do much to alleviate your guilt. There is great joy as you do not what comes naturally but what comes peacefully.

2. *Faith to do what you have chosen.* Many labor under the mistaken notion that once they choose what they believe are God's choices for them, the rest is easy. Actually, once you have chosen the right thing to do, the forces of hell may be unleashed against you to prevent you from following through with your good intentions.

The greatest hindrance to putting faith into action is fear. God often asks us to do things we do not know how to do. When this happens, fear is the natural result. People will suffer great pain rather than face the unknown by making changes they know they need to make. One college student said, "I know I can bear the pain the way I am. If I change, it might be more than I can bear." The result—a continued life of misery.

Recently I became lost while hiking in the rugged mountains of eastern Oregon. I started down a deep ravine that had a creek at the bottom. I believed that it was only a mile or so to the end of the ravine where I expected to find the main road to camp. I hiked on and on and soon it became completely dark. I was gripped by fear and the terrible feelings of being alone. I quoted Psalm 23 and sang hymns of God's closeness. This helped but I was still afraid. At one point I said, "God, I don't need your rod and staff for protection, but if you would just dilate my pupils a little so I can see better, I will be grateful." I trudged forward falling occasionally over rocks or logs.

At one point where the walls of the ravine were so steep I could hardly stand up, I reached my physical and psychological limit.

My body cried, "Stop!"

My mind said, "Go."

"I'll take a short cut," I heard my body say. "No," my mind countered. "You must stay by the creek. It is your only guide out of here."

I followed my mind, and about one hour later I ran right into a three-strand barbed wire fence. As I bounced off and checked to see that I wasn't injured, my heart rejoiced. I knew the fence was near the road. After carefully working my way through the fence I finally stumbled onto the roadbed. How beautiful those dim white tracks looked as they wound up the hill toward camp. "Thanks, God!" I said. "You are beautiful. You help those who aren't always smart enough to help themselves."

Faith conquered the fear which might have kept me lost for the rest of the night. While slowly making my way up the road, I realized what day it was and started to laugh. Without a doubt, this was my most scary Halloween. As I have relived this experience in my mind several times, I have realized that fear often keeps us from doing what we know we must do. There is probably a creek and a ravine in your life that needs to be followed. Faith is needed here too.

3. *Faith for strength to perform the task.* I often fail to do the right thing because of a second fear—a fear of being inadequate. Just as I am fearful of the unknown, I am also afraid of my own inadequacies. Tensely I watched my son, Mark, clinging to the rocks with his finger tips. I wondered when he would run out of strength and fall. How thankful I was for the mountaineering

instructors who stood alert and ready to tighten the safety rope! They shouted encouragement and gave instructions. They are like God, I thought. He helps us and encourages us even when we don't know if we have the strength or the skills for the task.

Mark kept listening to the instructions, and he made one climb after another. First the practice rock, then more advanced rocks. His faith in the instructors enabled him to use the natural abilities he had and to develop the courage to try new techniques and new challenges.

"It was super, Dad," he said. "Dave and Susan helped me a lot." How typical of God, I thought, always there when you need him. Faith says I can do the task because God is my enabler. I may not do it perfectly, but I will do it.

Spiritual Gifts and Doing

In recent years much attention has been given to the role of spiritual gifts. In general, this has been healthy as people have evaluated how God has gifted them to serve him more effectively. I will never forget hearing a deacon at our church share with a Bible study group that in his thirty years of being a Christian he had never felt worthwhile because he did not know how God had "gifted" him. A lady stood to her feet and said, "Oh, Dean, I'm so sorry. I have sat in your classes for many years, and I have never told you how gifted you are as a teacher."

Romans 12:3-8 emphasizes the importance of gifts and one of the pitfalls—pride—associated with awareness of gifts.

For by the grace given me I say to every one of you: Do not think of yourself more highly than you ought, but rather think of yourself with sober judgment, in accordance with the measure of faith God has given you. Just as each of us had one body with many members, and these members do not all have the same function, so in Christ we who are many form one body, and each member belongs to all the others. We have different gifts, according to the grace given us. If a man's gift is prophesying, let him use it in proportion to his faith. If it is serving, let

him serve; if it is teaching, let him teach; if it is encouraging, let him encourage; if it is contributing to the needs of others, let him give generously; if it is leadership, let him govern diligently; if it is showing mercy, let him do it cheerfully.
This passage is worth careful study to lock in our minds the interdependency we have on each other and the faith required to meet the needs of others.

Unfortunately, interdependency has eroded into a gunslinger mentality for many. People go around trying to collect evidence of their gifts, like notches on a gun, to convince others of their importance in the kingdom of God. Suddenly doing is no longer a matter of faith but of pride. Faith enables us to analyze our unique gifts and to develop outlets for those gifts for the purpose of serving the saints—not ourselves.

Hundreds of miserable people I have encountered are doing, doing, doing and yet never experiencing the joy of using the gifts they have been given. They do and do to prove they have worth rather than doing joyfully because they know they have worth to God. This tragedy has challenged me not to do anything that I cannot do joyfully. This does not mean that I will like doing everything God wants me to do. I may be fearful and, at times, I may be burdened. However, regardless of the circumstances, I can set my priorities and do with joyful anticipation what God allows me to do. I can joyfully say yes because without guilt I can joyfully say no. "And whatever you do, whether in word or deed, do it all in the name of the Lord Jesus, giving thanks to God the Father through him" (Col 3:17).

Our responsibility is to ask the question, How can my abilities and spiritual gifts best be used today? Spirituality is not a result of how gifted you are. It is a result of humbly using the spiritual gifts you have for the glory of God and for the well-being of others. Paul interrupted his long discussion of spiritual gifts in 1 Corinthins 12—14 to give us a poignant dissertation on love.

Eagerly desire the greater gifts. And now I will show you the most excellent way. If I speak in the tongues of men and of angels, but have not love, I am only a resounding gong or a clanging cymbal. If I have the gift of prophecy and can fathom all mysteries and all knowledge, and if I have a faith that can move mountains, but have not love, I am nothing. If I give all I possess to the poor and surrender my body to the flames, but have not love, I gain nothing. (1 Cor 12:31—13:3)

Love seeks a way to serve. Love is God in us bursting out to do, by faith, for others even when we are not sure they will be able to return the kindness. Love says, "Thanks, God, for helping me to do that even though I was reluctant." Using your gifts will enable you to understand more fully who you are and how important God is to your existence. A sharp bit isn't much good without power for the drill.

Motivation for Doing

Although Protestant Christianity has been characterized by an emphasis on the doctrine of grace, I have found a strong dualism that results in people doing because of fear that if they don't do, God will harm them. I mentioned this earlier when I referred to the belief in a God who zaps. Doctrinally, we believe that our position in Christ is secured by the work of Christ, but we sometimes act as though the permanence of that relationship is dependent on our works. We believe that we cannot do works that are sufficient to merit our salvation, but we act as though our works can somehow build security in our relationship with God.

This dualism dulls our ability to be discriminating in what we choose to do. If we are desperate to please God, we have trouble saying no. We do anything and everything that is available to do, and we allow urgent things to take the place of essential things. When we say yes, we feel guilty because we don't have confidence that we are doing what God wants us to do, and when we say no, we feel guilty and afraid God will zap us for turning him down. This horrible trap has resulted in many of God's people becoming either immobilized or bitter. Applying faith to our actions offers us a better alternative.

The Bible clearly states that we can know that we are God's children (Jn 20:31; 1 Jn 5:12). Knowing that we are one of God's loved ones is foundational. God does not play games with us. He wants us to know where we stand in his eyes. Paul emphasized this secure relationship by saying,

Who shall separate us from the love of Christ? Shall trouble or hardship or persecution or famine or nakedness or danger or sword? . . . No, in all these things we are more than conquerors through him who loved us. For I am convinced that neither death nor life, neither angels nor demons, neither the present nor the future, nor any powers, neither height nor depth, nor anything else in all creation, will be able to separate us from the love of God that is in Christ Jesus our Lord. (Rom 8:35, 37-39)

Hebrews says that because we know where we stand with God, we can be content. "Keep your lives free from the love of money and be content with what you have, because God has said, 'Never will I leave you; never will I forsake you' " (Heb 13:5). While conducting a study of emotions I became interested in the state of contentment. 1 Timothy 6:6, "Godliness with contentment is great gain," soon came to mind. As I meditated on this verse I became aware of the relationship between our emotional state and the quality of our life. The verse doesn't say godliness is great gain. It says godliness *with contentment* is great gain. Is it possible to miss the gains of a godly life because one is not content? I believe so. Many Christians who appear to be godly also appear to be miserable. Paul suggests a better way. We choose to be godly. I believe we must also choose to be content. How does contentment relate to our motivation for doing by faith?

The Greek word translated "contentment" is *autarkeia*. It means contentedness, competence, contentment of sufficiency. The implication is satisfaction with self or self-sufficiency. I was surprised to discover this definition because I had been taught that godliness and satisfaction with self should not be mentioned in the same breath. In 2 Corinthians 9:8 *autarkeia* is translated "having all that you need." The full verse reads, "And God is able to make all grace abound to you, so that in all things at all times, having all that you need, you will abound in every good work." The picture becomes clearer. God wants us to know that we are secure in him and that we have all that we need in him.

Security leads to self-satisfaction. What does self-satisfaction lead to? The verse concludes, "You will abound in every good work." Service, however, will not produce security. Those who serve to gain security are not acting out of faith and consequently will be frustrated. The only productive motivation for doing is our position in Christ and our awareness that in him we have all we need.

Obstacles to Doing

We have seen the goal. Now we must consider some common psychological and spiritual hurdles which may be encountered. These are our enemies.

Feelings of inferiority, which stand between us and doing by faith, are common among believers. Inferiority says, "I do not have all that I need to live successfully." Faith says, "God the enabler has enabled me and will enable me to do what he wants me to do." As we read, "Having all that you need, you will abound in every good work" (2 Cor 9:8).

You may say, "But I don't just *feel* inferior. I *am* inferior." True, you may be. But God isn't. Your feelings of inferiority spring from comparing yourself with others or the ideals of a perfectionistic, superstar society. This is not God's plan. Our great God delights in using the weak and the humble to shame the mighty, even the superstars (see 1 Cor 1:27-28). "If [better translated, *since*] God is for us, who can be against us?" (Rom 8:31). We are dealing with more than just positive thinking. We are dealing with a God who wants to empower you to do that which you may feel unable to do.

If you want to grow in this area, pause and select one thing that you have been putting off because of your feelings of inferiority. Commit this to God and then do it, knowing that he enables you.

You will have success (not perfection) as you take courage and trust God. The feelings of inferiority, which are always a broad and inaccurate generalization, will give way to a more realistic picture of your strengths and weaknesses. You will gain a continuous awareness of God's presence even when you are weak.

A second obstacle, related to the first, is one we considered in the chapter on self-esteem—perfectionism. Not only does it diminish our view of ourselves, it also diminishes our ability to act. God is the only person who can do perfectly. God wants us to do as well as we can, and then to leave the consequences to him. We are not to be immobilized because we feel we are flawed. As believers we are to have high standards but not impossible ones.

Can you imagine how frustrated a man would be if he tried to give his wife a perfect kiss? How would he know if his lips were pursed just right? How would he know he couldn't do better? Think of all the joy he would miss if he waited for perfection to kiss her.

God takes our actions and adds his touch of blessing or perfection. "I planted the seed, Apollos watered it, but God made it grow" (1 Cor 3:6). Ecclesiastes 11:1 says, "Cast your bread upon the waters, for after many days you will find it again." I believe this is true of doing by faith. As we do, God blesses our actions, and our doing improves. If we don't act, God can't bless.

A brilliant friend of mine, a university professor, never published any of her ideas or research. Why? She was a perfectionist. Not only did she lose out, but others did not have the advantage of her work either. If you struggle in this area, *do* now and evaluate later. Otherwise you will never experience the joy of doing.

A third obstacle to doing by faith is escapism. Because we are afraid of failure, on the one hand, and seek immediate gratification from what we do, on the other, we escape. If I have some baking to do I may escape by watching TV. As long as I watch TV, no one will say I have made a bad pie. This will feel right because of the immediate gratification (or at least passification) that comes from TV. The problem is that this pattern catches up with us.

Procrastination and escapism lead to further escapism which then leads to failure, feelings of guilt and depression.

Escapism usually puts us into an unreal world, a world of pleasure without pain, a world of instant success. The drawback is that we never grow. We never experience God's power or self-satisfaction. We may escape through video games, TV, drugs, alcohol, movies, sports or even Bible studies. Many Christians attend so many Bible studies that they never have time to practice the wonderful things they are learning. Escapism is like a helium balloon. The balloon may allow you to soar for a time, but when the helium seeps out, you are left flat.

A fourth obstacle to doing by faith is boredom, a product of a highly technological and automated society. "I have tried it all, and there isn't much left to do," or so we tell ourselves. Boredom, however, is a choice we make. Those same old things may be exciting if we choose to look for the excitement in them.

Boredom sets in when I lose sight of my purpose or when I cease to savor the pleasure of the activity. Boredom is not a condition like being out of gas. It is a perception or a value judgment, like saying, "I don't think I have enough gas to get there."

The impressions of others can also drastically affect our views. Did you ever notice what often happens when someone comes up to you while you are performing a menial task and says, "Isn't this boring?" You may have been enjoying the job or at least tolerating it well, but you will immediately lose interest.

When we feel bored we may also begin to catastrophize by saying, "It is awful that this isn't fun and exciting." Yet the fact is that life does not consist of doing only pleasurable things. We need to look for satisfaction even in repetitive tasks.

One helpful question I ask myself is, "Who am I doing this for?" If I am cleaning the garage (a potentially boring task), I will ask who will benefit from this: me, Sandy, the children or who? I like all these people, so continuing to clean is easier, knowing that the clean garage has the potential to make all these people happy. This is more than just a gimmick. I am analyzing an event in terms of purpose rather than just the routine.

I once met a church janitor who was excited about his job. I asked him how he handled the boredom of doing the same thing over and over each week. He said, "It's not the same old thing. Each week is an opportunity to do something for God." He turned a potentially boring task into an opportunity for worship.

Boredom in and of itself will not prevent doing by faith. It remains an obstacle only when we tell ourselves that we cannot go on because we are bored. Who says you cannot continue to do what you need to do because you are bored? Boredom says, "Stop! The pleasure is gone." Faith says, "Continue! The reward is just around the corner." As Galatians 6:9 says, "Let us not become weary in doing good, for at the proper time we will reap a harvest if we do not give up."

We will not escape boredom altogether. Such is the substance of life. The question is, Will boredom control us? The choice is ours.

Clearly, the four obstacles to doing by faith that we have discussed are not all that we will face. We will experience numerous fears and frustrations. Were it not for these obstacles, we wouldn't need to apply faith at all. They provide us with the opportunity to put God to the test and to see how faithful he is when we trust him.

Risks, Realism and Rewards

How can we keep on the track of applying faith to doing? First, recognize that taking risks is part of life. Anything you do might fail. However, as God enables you, things may turn out better than you imagined. As I have worked with the chapter leaders of Inter-Varsity Christian Fellowship I easily recognize the things God can help them do. But as these leaders take the risk of trusting God, they seem surprised at the positive outcomes. From my point of view, their success isn't surprising at all. God loves to help us use the abilities he has given us.

Second, set reachable goals. There is nothing more frustrating than struggling at an impossible task. On the other hand, rarely is anything impossible if you break it down into small attainable steps. Writing a term paper may be impossible, but writing a sentence or a paragraph is not. If I set my goal at finishing a paragraph and then at writing another, I will proceed with feelings of success. If I look only at the entire project, I may become discouraged. I often set minimum goals which I will reach and then bonus goals which I may work toward if things go unexpectedly well.

We are much more apt to succumb to Murphy's Law when we have overloaded ourselves with goals that are not realistic. If our goals aren't attainable and then something does go wrong, we become doubly frustrated because we have no chance for success. If our goals have been reachable in the first place, we may put in the extra effort when something goes wrong and still succeed.

Managing reinforcements is a third help to getting things done. Reward yourself after you have reached your goal and not before. Do your work before your favorite activity, not after. If you wait until afterward, you may never get to the task.

If you enjoy football games on Saturday but have a Sunday-school class to teach on Sunday, allow yourself to watch the game only after you have finished your preparation. You will do the preparation faster and maybe even better because you will be less tired than preparing after the game. You will also enjoy the game more because you will not worry about the class.

Sticking to such plans is difficult for us because we live in a society of such abundance. We are used to getting most everything we want. We must learn to be tougher on ourselves and take our goals seriously. If you are trying to diet, reinforcing yourself with food is possible. But going out to eat on Saturday night with a friend must be contingent on keeping your diet Sunday through Friday.

You may also need to manage the consequences. Don't be afraid to put some pressure on yourself. If you want to stop procrastinating, you may need to establish a meaningful negative consequence for not reaching your goals. A friend of mine establishes checkpoints which he has to reach en route to his goal. For each checkpoint he gives a friend a $20 bill. The friend is asked to burn a bill each time the checkpoint is not reached. This may sound radical, but in all the years he has done this he has lost only one $20 bill. This is a small price to pay for years of success. We can accomplish more than we ever dreamed if we are willing to take our rewards after we finish our work and not before.

A fourth practical help is to keep company with people who respect your goals and are disciplined themselves. When Nehemiah was rebuilding the walls of Jerusalem, he was repeatedly confronted by people who distracted him from his task. Nehemiah listened to them long enough to be sure that what they were saying wasn't more important than his primary task. "I sent messengers to them with this reply: 'I am carrying on a great project and cannot go down. Why should the work stop while I leave it and go down to you?' Four times they sent me the same message, and each time I gave them the same answer" (Neh 6:3-4). He went full speed ahead with the work God had called him to do.

We do not need friends who keep us from our primary purpose in life. We do not need activities which keep us from our family or from worship. Sometimes we pay much too high a price for trying to be all things to all people.

I have made a strong plea for setting priorities because I don't believe our actions can please God unless, by faith, we do so. Our priorities, of course, are not God's priorities if they make us insensitive to the needs of those around us. When activities become more important than people or than God, we have lost sight of what is important.

Faith-controlled doing is doing that comes out of the abundance of knowing that God loves us and has equipped us to do all that he wants us to do. Regardless of the obstacles, he will meet our needs.

14
Thriving Faith

GOD WANTS US TO LIVE BY FAITH because living by faith is living with him. He wants our whole person—our thinking, feeling, choosing and doing. As I have contended throughout this book, Hebrews 11:6 must be applied to all areas of our person. "Without faith it is impossible to please God." In this final chapter we will look at the way faith in each of the four areas of our personality combines in three important aspects of faith: believing faith, thinking faith and multiplying faith.

Believing Faith
Believing faith brings us into a relationship with God. This is the essence of the new birth by which we become God's sons and daughters. Paul wrote to the Romans that this is "the word of

faith we are proclaiming: That if you confess with your mouth, 'Jesus is Lord,' and believe in your heart that God raised him from the dead, you will be saved. For it is with your heart that you believe and are justified, and it is with your mouth that you confess and are saved" (Rom 10:8-10). Faith involves both thought and action, says Paul.

Faith in God has content. Believing faith says the historic person Jesus Christ of Nazareth lived, died and was raised from the dead by God. His death has been accepted by God as full payment for my sins. I accept his payment on my behalf and acknowledge that, because of this act of love, I can confidently and comfortably rest as a member of God's family. I am a child of God because Jesus Christ has purchased my membership back into God's family and I have willingly accepted his gift to me.

Romans 10:8-10 also emphasizes the feelings that accompany the thoughts. The phrase "believe in your heart" has reference to a combination of both. When Peter preached to thousands on the day of Pentecost, "they were cut to the heart" (Acts 2:37). "Then they that gladly received his word were baptized" (Acts 2:41 KJV). Belief encompasses the full range of emotions from deep grief to great gladness. The Ethiopian converted and baptized by Philip also "went on his way rejoicing" (Acts 8:39).

Believing faith brings together thinking and feeling through the mechanism of choice. Deuteronomy 30:11-20 (which is the background passage referred to in Rom 10:6-8) highlights this issue. Moses commands the people to love God, an act which is neither too difficult for them nor out of their reach. The point of the passage comes in verse 19: "This day I call heaven and earth as witnesses against you that I have set before you life and death, blessings and curses. Now choose life, so that you and your children may live and that you may love the LORD your God, listen to his voice, and hold fast to him."

I remember explaining the gospel to a fellow faculty member when I was a beginning professor. He asked good questions, so I knew his thinking was straight. He acknowledged his need, so I felt the Holy Spirit was wooing him. Yet when the time came to choose, he said no. I was stunned! His thinking and feeling were in line. His choosing, however, was not. Ten years later I learned that through the friendship and faithful witness of a mutual family friend he had made a new choice. This time he said yes. The essence of believing faith is saying yes to God.

Romans 10:8-10 also gives us something to do in our believing. "It is with your mouth that you confess and are saved." Saying yes to God transforms our choice into a reality. When the jailer asked Paul and Silas, "Men, what must I do to be saved?" they did not correct him by saying, "You should have asked, 'What must I think, feel and choose to be saved.'" They said, "Believe in the Lord Jesus, and you will be saved" (Acts 16:30-31).

Thinking Faith
The Gospels of Matthew, Mark and Luke each record the parable of the sower. In it the seed, which represents the Word of God, did not thrive and grow in all the soils it was planted in. In one instance, the seed was taken away before it could start to grow. In the second soil the seed sprouted but did not take root. In the third the seed grew but was later crowded out by other things. In the last soil the seed grew and produced a high yield. So not all people respond in belief to God's Word in the same way. But this parable clearly indicates that for those who do respond, believing faith is not the end of faith but only the beginning.

What are the characteristics of a faith which thrives and produces a high yield? It is a faith that is integrated into every aspect of our person, unifying us as individuals. Thriving faith recognizes that God is with us on a moment-by-moment basis. Thriving faith believes that God is present, available and interested in every aspect of our person, *every aspect of our person*. Since he is concerned about our thinking, feeling, choosing and doing he can make us integrated beings. We don't have to remain unbalanced, fragmented or painfully dualistic. When I am trusting God in the feeling area, I am freer to think greater thoughts, make more difficult choices and even do what otherwise might seem impossible. Likewise, faith in any of the other areas affects the potential for faith in the remaining three.

Believing that God is present, available and interested in every aspect of our person is not a once-and-for-all matter. It is a process. It is a process of affirming that what God says is true, of allowing our feelings to be absorbed by this great truth, of making choices based on that truth and then of acting in accordance with that truth. This requires discipline. This requires that we bring errant thoughts into line with scriptural truth. This requires that we choose to focus on what is positive in life rather than indulge in feelings that would cause us to deny God's presence. This requires that we choose life rather than death.

This process is a spiritual battle, a battle over whether to choose right or wrong, a battle of faith to overcome fear, to overcome procrastination, to try to do what we are not sure we can do, to believe that God is the One who enables us to do. Thriving faith is faith in action. It trusts God for something each day.

The parable of the sower says that some of the seeds do not mature because "they are choked by life's worries, riches and pleasures" (Lk 8:14). Faith in our feelings can keep us from choking on worry. Faith in God who meets our physical needs can keep us from getting hung up on wealth. Faith in an ever-present God can help us to choose permanent pleasure rather than the pleasures of sin which last only for a short time (Heb 11:25). David, who himself made some bad choices, wrote, "You have made known to me the path of life; you will fill me with joy in your presence, with eternal pleasures at your right hand" (Ps 16:11).

Thriving faith is responsible faith. It clearly and deliberately seeks to expose our level of trust in God. Thriving faith is ever-conscious of the opportunity to experience God in new and exciting ways. May I suggest that you think seriously about the positive impact that this type of growing faith can have on your life day by day? A friend said, "When I walk with God, I am not so alone and I don't feel so confused. I even get optimistic once in a while."

Multiplying Faith

When we allow God to touch our lives and we experience living by faith daily, our lives touch others. We can't stop it. I remember how amazed I was when, as a beginning university professor, students would come up after class and say, "You must be a believer." I was unaware of teaching anything other than the subject at hand. Subsequently, I have learned that the tracks of God across our lives are apparent to those who observe us. A student came to me for counseling about "religion." I warned him that I could not be unbiased in that area. His response took me off guard. "I know," he said respectfully. "That's why I chose you instead of someone who doesn't appear to know God."

Believing faith which is allowed to thrive will become a faith which multiplies. Express your faith in both word and deed. It is exciting to live in relationship with a God who brings healing to sick people living in a sick society. God has something to offer you, and you have something to offer to others.

Notes

Chapter 2: Your Whole Self
[1]Os Guinness, *In Two Minds* (Downers Grove, Ill.: InterVarsity Press, 1976), p. 67.
[2]Phillip J. Swihart, *How to Live with Your Feelings* (Downers Grove, Ill.: InterVarsity Press, 1972), p. 12.
[3]Susan K. Gilmore, *The Counselor-in-Training* (Englewood Cliffs, N.J.: Prentice-Hall, 1973), p. 47.

Chapter 3: The Balanced Life
[1]Gordon McMinn, *Taking Charge* (Denver, Accent, 1980), p. 16.
[2]Paul Welter, *Family Problems and Predicaments: How to Respond* (Wheaton, Ill.: Tyndale, 1977), p. 212.
[3]Paul A. Hauck, *How to Stand Up for Yourself* (Philadelphia: Westminster, 1979), editor's comment on the cover of the book.

Chapter 4: The Undivided Life
[1]Guinness, *In Two Minds,* p. 128.
[2]Swihart, *How to Live with Your Feelings.*

Chapter 5: The Faith-Filled Life
[1]C. H. Spurgeon quoted in J. I. Packer, *Knowing God* (Downers Grove, Ill.: InterVarsity Press, 1973), p. 13.
[2]Guinness, *In Two Minds,* p. 97.

Chapter 6: Thoughtful Faith
[1]John R. W. Stott, *Your Mind Matters* (Downers Grove, Ill.: InterVarsity Press, 1972), p. 20.
[2]Philip Yancey and Tim Stafford, *Unhappy Secrets of the Christian Life* (Grand Rapids: Zondervan, 1979), p. 8.
[3]Guinness, *In Two Minds,* p. 115.
[4]Stott, *Your Mind Matters,* p. 36.

[5]Bill and Gloria Gaither, "I Am a Promise."
[6]Stott, *Your Mind Matters,* p. 41.

Chapter 7: Managing Emotional Investments
[1]Frank B. Minirth and Paul D. Meier, *Happiness Is a Choice* (Grand Rapids: Baker, 1978).
[2]Swihart, *How to Live with Your Feelings,* p. 19.
[3]Nancy Anne Smith, *All I Need Is Love* (Downers Grove, Ill.: InterVarsity Press, 1977).
[4]Ellis and Harper, *A Guide to Rational Living* (Englewood Cliffs, N.J.: Prentice-Hall, 1961), p. 168.
[5]Swihart, *How to Live with Your Feelings.*
[6]S. Bruce Narramore, *You're Someone Special* (Grand Rapids: Zondervan, 1978), p. 153.
[7]Ronald Barclay Allen, *Praise! A Matter of Life and Breath* (Nashville: Thomas Nelson, 1980), p. 243.
[8]Swihart, *How to Live with Your Feelings,* pp. 53-54.
[9]David Augsburger, *Caring Enough to Confront* (Glendale, Calif.: Regal, 1973), pp. 165-66.
[10]Swihart, *How to Live with Your Feelings,* p. 57.

Chapter 8: Anger without Sin: Keys to Emotional Control
[1]Paul A. Hauck, *Overcoming Frustration and Anger* (Philadelphia: Westminster, 1974), chap. 3.
[2]Welter, *Family Problems,* p. 103.
[3]Robert E. Alberti, and Michael L. Emmons, *Your Perfect Right,* 3rd ed. (San Luis Obispo, Calif.: Impact, 1978), pp. 11-12.
[4]McMinn, public address.
[5]Melba Colgrove, Harold H. Bloomfield and Peter McWilliams, *How to Survive the Loss of a Love* (New York: Bantam, 1976), p. 86.
[6]David Augsburger, *Caring Enough to Forgive* (Glendale, Calif.: Regal, 1981), pp. 52-53.

Chapter 10: Self-Esteem: God Don't Make No Junk
[1]Charles Swindoll, *For Those Who Hurt* (Portland: Multnomah, 1977), n. pag.
[2]Narramore, *You're Someone Special,* p. 133.
[3]John Powell, *Unconditional Love* (Niles, Ill.: Argus, 1978), p. 68.
[4]Paul A. Hauck, *How to Do What You Want to Do* (Philadelphia: Westminster, 1976), p. 46.
[5]Nathaniel Branden, *The Psychology of Self-Esteem* (New York: Bantam, 1969), p. 127.

[6]Karen Horney, *The Neurotic Personality of Our Time* (New York: W. W. Norton, 1937), pp. 234-35.
[7]Narramore, *You're Someone Special,* p. 87.
[8]Eric Berne, *Games People Play* (New York: Grove Press, 1964).

Chapter 11: Choosing Emotions and Other Important Decisions
[1]Donald Meichenbaum, "Cognitive Behavioral Therapy," public address at Norfolk Regional Center, Nebraska, 1976.
[2]Guinness, *In Two Minds,* p. 39.

Chapter 12: Resolving Responsibility
[1]David Augsburger, *Caring Enough to Forgive—Caring Enough Not to Forgive* (Scottdale, Pa.: Herald, 1981), p. 42.
[2]Paul A. Hauck, *Overcoming Worry and Fear* (Philadelphia: Westminster, 1975), p. 53.